This book was donated

to

Joseph T. Walker School

1984

by

Hetal Joshi

John F. Kennedy

America's Youngest President

Illustrated by Al Fiorentino

John F. Kennedy

America's Youngest President

by Lucy Post Frisbee

Illustrated by Al Fiorentino

THE BOBBS-MERRILL COMPANY, INC.
INDIANAPOLIS/NEW YORK

PUBLISHED BY THE BOBBS-MERRILL CO., INC.

INDIANAPOLIS/NEW YORK

MANUFACTURED IN THE UNITED STATES OF AMERICA

Library of Congress Cataloging in Publication Data

Frisbee, Lucy Post
  John F. Kennedy, America's youngest president.

  (Childhood of famous Americans)
  Summary: A biography focusing on the childhood of the youngest
man ever elected President.
  1. Kennedy, John F. (John Fitzgerald), *1917–1963*—Juvenile
literature.
  2. Presidents—United States—Biography—Juvenile literature.

  [1. Kennedy, John F. (John Fitzgerald), *1917–1963.*
  2. Presidents] I. Title. II. Series.
E842.Z9P67   973.922'092'4   [B]   82-45451
ISBN 0-672-52737-5 (pbk.)   [92]   AACR2

TO
Rose Fitzgerald Kennedy
who instilled in her son,
John Fitzgerald Kennedy,
the love and loyalty
to God and Country
which made him
a great and good American,
the President of these United States

The author is deeply grateful to the following: the members of the family of President Kennedy, particularly Mrs. Joseph P. Kennedy, Mrs. R. Sargent Shriver, Mrs. John B. Value III, and Thomas A. Fitzgerald; to his lifelong friend, K. LeMoyne Billings; his Latin master at Canterbury, Philip Brodie; the Headmaster of The Choate School, Seymour St. John, and members of the Choate faculty who knew JFK as boy and man—Earl A. Leinbach, Owen H. Morgan, Mr. and Mrs. Courtenay Hemenway, and Hubert S. Packard; Wilton B. Crosby Jr. of Wianno fame; Colonel George A. Lincoln, USMA; Erwin D. Canham, Editor of The Christian Science Monitor; Harry Harcher, Editor of Boys' Life; White House Press Secretary George E. Reedy, and President Lyndon B. Johnson. Permission granted to quote from: Boys' Life and The Christian Science Monitor.

Illustrations

Full pages

Numerous smaller illustrations

Contents

Books by Lucy Post Frisbee

BRIGHAM YOUNG: COVERED WAGON BOY
  (with Polly Carver Jordan)
JOHN BURROUGHS: BOY OF FIELD AND STREAM

★ # John F.
Kennedy

America's Youngest President

Fireworks on the Fourth

THUMP! Thud! Whack! The two boys traded savage blows. Pounding, punching, poking, they fought their way from one side of the lawn to the other. A jab here, a sock there. A belt to the right, a clout to the left. First one was on top, then the other.

Finally, the smaller boy found himself spread-eagled on the ground, his scrawny arms pinned down, his slight frame wriggling furiously as he tried to free himself.

"Give up, Jack?"

"Don't be silly," Jack gasped. "Of course I won't give up. Not if you clobber me all day."

"Don't you know when you're licked?"

"Who says I'm licked?" Jack's nose was bloody, one eye swollen shut, his face streaked with dirt. "I'm not licked. I'm resting."

The three little girls on the sidelines were watching the scuffle with mixed feelings. Kick was excited and even four-year-old Eunice was watching the battle, but their oldest sister, Rosemary, didn't like to see anyone get hurt. In spite of the noise of combat, baby Patricia was still sleeping soundly in her carriage.

"Get up, Jack," Kick urged her brother. "Don't let Joe beat you again! Smash him!"

"Smash him!" Eunice echoed.

"Smash him!" Joe Jr. repeated in disgust. "Who do you silly girls think he is? Jack Dempsey? Just because his name is Jack doesn't mean he can fight like the heavyweight champ. Remember this Jack is named Kennedy!'"

"Better let him up, Joe," Rosemary warned.

"Here comes Mother. You know how she feels about you boys scrapping."

The boys were still sprawled out on the grass as Mrs. Kennedy rounded the corner.

"Boys!" She stared in dismay. "Fighting *again!* And in your best clothes. You were all dressed up to go into the city with your grandfather and now look at you!"

The boys' white shirts were all grass stained. She knew their knickers would never come clean. Dirt and grime covered their faces and their hands were filthy.

Mrs. Kennedy shook her head. "I'm afraid there'll be no Fourth of July celebration for either one of you. No parade, no ball game, no fireworks——"

"Mother," Jack tried to explain. "Joe really didn't mean any harm. I dared him and he took the dare, that's all."

"That's all, Mother." Joe put a friendly arm

around his brother's shoulders. "We won't get in another fight. We promise."

"Not for another five minutes, I presume." Her voice was stern but there was a slight twinkle in her eye. "I'll give you boys one more chance to behave. Clean up in a hurry. Your grandfather is due here now. And remember, boys, if there is any more quarreling you'll both see fireworks, but," she added in a warning tone, "they won't be the kind that celebrates the Fourth of July!"

By midmorning, the boys were feeding the pigeons on Boston Common and waiting with their grandfather for the parade to start. On the gravel paths through the Public Gardens, the nursemaids wheeled their young charges in prams. Small boys tore by on their three-wheelers. Quaint elderly ladies, unmistakably from Beacon Hill, primly took their daily walk along the edges of the pond.

14

The Swan Boats looked cool and inviting as they sailed quietly along on the willow-fringed lagoon.

"Could we have a ride?" Jack asked.

"Sissy stuff," Joe Jr. said. "For *girls*."

"If the Swan Boats are for girls, how come all those other boys are taking rides?" Jack asked. "They're bigger than you, Joe!"

"Swan Boat rides are for everybody—the young, the old, and the in-between." Grandpa Fitzgerald beamed with remembered joys. "I was just a little tyke when my mother first took me for a ride on the Swan Boats. And it seems only yesterday that your mother was a tiny girl riding along in these very same boats. They have been a part of Boston for a good many years."

"How do they work?" Joe asked curiously. "Don't see any oars."

"There aren't any oars, Joe."

"There aren't any sails, either," Jack said. "And

15

there's no noise—no vibration—no motor—nothing——"

"Must move by magic," their grandpa said.

"Don't be so mysterious, Grandpa," Joe said impatiently. "Tell us how they run."

"The drivers pedal them like bicycles."

"That's why the boats move so silently." Jack added, "Why, they're just like the barges of King Arthur's Day, aren't they?"

"Don't ask us, Sir Galahad," Joe replied. "You're the one who is always reading about King Arthur and his noble knights."

Across the Common, tentative drumbeats and horn tootings of the band could be heard.

"Hear that, boys? The band is warming up. Wait another day for a Swan Boat ride, Jack. You don't want to be out in the middle of the pond when the parade starts." Mr. Fitzgerald pulled his watch out of his vest pocket and held it to his ear. He shook his head. Then he shook

16

the watch. "Jack, my time-piece has stopped again. Run over and ask that policeman the correct hour."

"What policeman, Grandpa?"

"Yonder by Washington's statue."

Jack took off on a run, while Joe Jr. and his grandfather watched the crowds gather along the street.

"Ah, this is a great day, Joe. It's Uncle Sam's birthday and everybody in America ought to be celebrating. Old John Adams had the right idea. He always said the Fourth of July should be a day of public rejoicing. Flags should wave, he said. Ring bells, fire the cannons, beat drums, and blow bugles!"

"Jack and I have been firing the cannons, all right," Joe said with a grin. "We were up before dawn, shooting off firecrackers."

"You boys will be worn out before the fracas begins. What kind of fireworks do you have?"

"Jack and I wanted to get the biggest noise for the money——"

"Naturally," his grandfather agreed.

"So we bought torpedoes. We really wanted to get some of those five- or six-inchers, but we didn't dare. You know how Mother and the girls are about noisy firecrackers. Wish Dad could have been home for the Fourth," Joe added wistfully. "It would be fun to shoot off the fireworks with him."

"Once his business affairs in New York and Hollywood are settled, your father'll be able to spend more time with you. He misses you just as much as you miss him," Grandpa Fitz said sympathetically. "I'll be glad to help you boys set off your fireworks. Did you buy anything besides the noisy type? You know your grandmother likes fancy ones."

"We had to get sparklers for the girls, of course. *Sparklers!*" Joe growled the word.

"Sparklers seem tame to you boys?"

"I'll say they do. Jack and I managed to get a few skyrockets and Roman candles though," he added. "I like skyrockets best. They're the most dangerous."

"Oh, I don't know." His grandfather gave a chuckle. "You put Jack behind a Roman candle and it can get mighty hazardous."

"Where is Jack, anyhow? You suppose he got lost over there?"

"Nonsense! An eight-year-old boy lost on Boston Common? *Could* happen, I suppose, but not if that boy is John Fitzgerald Kennedy. After all, you were both born and bred right here in Boston. And both sides of your family, too. Why, your mother first saw the light of day just a stone's throw from Paul Revere's house, and your Grandfather Kennedy once knew every square foot of this city—and just about every voter in it."

19

"Not to mention our other grandfather!"

"Modesty forbids me——" Grandpa paused.

"Mayor of Boston for three—count 'em—three terms!" Half laughing, Joe gave a low sweeping bow. "And the first Irishman to be so elected!"

A blare of trumpets and a roll of drums interrupted. The parade was about to begin.

"Where's Jack!" Joe Jr. was concerned.

"Right here, Joe!" Jack was breathless from running. "When I heard that band, Grandpa, I came back lickety-split."

"What took you so long?"

"I forgot what you sent me for, Grandpa," Jack said sheepishly. "There was a hurdy-gurdy on the other side of the Common with a cute monkey. I guess I sort of followed them. It was half the music and half the monkey. I forgot to watch where I was going and wound up way over on Tremont Street."

"You'd forget your head if it wasn't fastened to your shoulders," Joe said.

"Maybe so, but I won't forget what I just saw over in the Old Granary Grounds." Jack's face was aglow. "It was like walking right inside a history book to see those famous names on the headstones."

"Boston *is* a history book," his grandfather said. "Yankee Doodle town itself."

"I recognized almost all of the names on the headstones over there. Paul Revere, Samuel Adams, John Hancock. Even Benjamin Franklin's mother and father are buried there. But, Grandpa, who was Crispus Attucks?"

"Attucks? Crispus Attucks? Let me think." For a moment, Mr. Fitzgerald seemed stumped. Then he smiled delightedly. "Ah, I remember. He was the first man killed in the Revolution, Jack. Shot at the Boston Massacre, way back in 1770. Interesting, too, because he really didn't have much to fight for. He was a Negro without any home or family. Yet he was the first person to die in the Revolution."

Just then a shout went up from the crowd. "Here comes the parade!"

The boys and their grandfather edged toward the scene. "Grandpa," Jack said, "I bet you used to ride in the parades when you were the Mayor of Boston."

"That I did, Jack, and proudly, too."

First came four of Boston's finest—brawny, stalwart policemen marching jauntily along.

"How can they stand those long coats on a sweltering day like this?" Jack asked.

"Because they've Irish blood in their veins, and in Boston the Irish have learned to stand anything." Grandpa seemed to be joking, but there was a half-serious look in his eyes.

Next came the band. The tuba player seemed to have a note for each foot as he marched along. Oom-pah! Oompah! Left, right, left!

The drummer was an artist. He crossed his sticks in the air, waved to the crowd, and never even missed a beat.

Someone lit a package of Chinese firecrackers and tossed them neatly into the tuba. The oom-pah was so loud that the tuba player didn't hear the explosions, but when smoke began to filter out through his walrus moustache, he stopped to investigate.

The crowd went wild with laughter.

After the patriotic floats passed by with many an "oh" and "ah" from the spectators, the Civil War veterans marched down the parade route together, side by side. There were still more than a dozen of them, dressed in the blue uniforms of the Union Army, their campaign hats gleaming with golden cords. They got a big hand. So did the veterans of the Spanish-American War. But when the young fellows who had come back from "Over There" stepped along in their high-collared khaki uniforms with knee breeches and rolled puttees, they got a rousing welcome.

"Look, Joe," Jack pointed excitedly, "next come the Boy Scouts. A couple of years and you can march with them." He added wistfully, "Four more years for me to wait."

A line of cars ended the parade, along with some of Boston's regular horse-drawn vehicles. Most of the cars were new, others were older models, but all were fancy, polished and quite splendid to behold.

The boys knew the cars by heart. They called out the names as the machines drove by.

There was a new Cadillac touring car, then an Auburn. A majestic Deusenberg rolled by, then an air-cooled Franklin, its comic-looking hood drawing wisecracks from the spectators. A Chalmers with a body as big as a whaleboat went by, and an older Stanley Steamer quietly hissed along the route.

There was a Pierce Arrow, then a Stutz Bearcat, then a LaSalle with pigskin upholstery. A Cunningham speedster and a Marmon six-cylinder followed.

"Wish we had a car with a rumble seat," Joe said. "Look at that Reo Flying Cloud!"

25

"Humph, isn't your father's Rolls Royce good enough for you, Joe?"

"It's *too* good, Grandpa. I like our Ford just as much, but I wish we had something speedy looking. Like that Packard roadster." Joe's eyes were wide with admiration.

"Can't beat the Lincoln for my money," his grandfather said. "Henry Ford must think so, too. He's just bought the Lincoln Company."

"You mean the same Henry Ford that built our Tin Lizzie?" Jack asked.

"One and the same," Mr. Fitzgerald replied. "Wonder what old Henry is going to do with an elegant car like the Lincoln? That Police Flyer is some different from the Model T."

"Look, Grandpa! Here come the horses. Do you suppose there'll be a runaway?"

"There usually is, Jack. Never saw a Fourth of July parade without one!"

Red, white, and blue bunting covered the huge

boxlike milk wagons. An S.S. Pierce delivery truck was drawn by a team of dappled grays. In the sunlight, their harness brasses gleamed gold as the spirited horses pranced along.

The Bay State Livery Stable had a huge float. Its fleet of horses and wagons delivered coal and ice, milk, and newspapers to all of Boston. An ice wagon went by, covered with canvas like an old-fashioned prairie schooner.

Then it happened—the runaway that everyone expected and the boys secretly hoped for!

There was a thunder of hoofs, a volley of shouts, and a crowd of running men and boys. A horse galloped down Charles Street and turned the corner right at the entrance to the Public Gardens. The buggy he was pulling smashed against the high granite curb.

Traces snapped. The horse was flung free. With a delighted whinny, the animal lifted his head to the breeze and took off at a gallop.

The parade was officially over!

Later that afternoon, the heat settled down over Fenway Park like a thick blanket, leaving Jack limp and lazy. A faint breath of air stirred under the trees by the bleachers.

The five hot dogs he had gulped so hurriedly began to stir uneasily in his stomach. So did the eight paper cups of pink lemonade. When the vendor with the cones of cotton candy went by, Jack had to turn his eyes away. Gruesome, he thought. He gulped and wished he'd skipped that third ice-cream.

The sound of his grandfather's cheerful voice broke in on his misery. "Oh-h-h—take—me—out to—the—bal-l-l-l game!"

"Grandpa!" Jack interrupted him with a huge grin. "The only tune you're supposed to know is 'Sweet Adeline'!"

"That's for my voting public, Jack. But it's not the song for Fenway Park when a double-header is about to begin." Honey Fitz looked around with a delighted smile. "So the Washington Senators are pitting their championship strength against our Boston Pilgrims——"

"No! Grandpa, you've just got to remember!" Joe shook his head. "It isn't the Boston Pilgrims any more. Now it's the Red Sox."

"Maybe," his grandfather replied, slightly disgruntled. "But just the same I can remember the Pilgrims."

"You *can*, Grandpa?" Jack had a wink for him. "That's three hundred years!"

"Jack, you've got a good sense of humor." His grandfather looked at him seriously. "Don't ever lose it."

The Senators may have been the champions of the American League, but they still lost to Boston in the first game of that double-header on the Fourth of July in 1925. But in the second game, their Bucky Harris knocked a home run over the left field fence and Washington leaped ahead with a score of 5 to 1.

The game ended with the Senators dividing scores with the Red Sox and with Mr. Fitzgerald taking his grandsons to the Boston dugout.

The pitcher for the Red Sox, Howard Ehmke, had a hearty welcome for the boys and their grandfather. "Howdy, Mr. Fitzgerald. Going to sing us a tune? We need to cheer up after losing that one."

"You pitched a great game, Mr. Ehmke," Joe Jr. said. "The Senators just got four runs."

"And the Pilgrims came through with seven!" Grandpa Fitz added cheerily.

"Grandpa!" Jack whispered. "Remember what Joe told you. It's not the Pilgrims now."

"My boy," and his grandfather drew himself up as tall as his short frame could reach, "my boy, when I was Mayor of Boston, I used to throw out the first ball of the season. I can remember the Boston Pilgrims from those days, and the Red Sox is too new-fangled for me."

"The Pilgrims was a good name for a Boston team," Howard Ehmke said.

"Glad somebody agrees with me, Mr. Ehmke! And now, these grandsons of mine want to have their score cards autographed if your arm isn't too tired from all that pitching."

"Never too tired to sign my name for you, Mr. Fitzgerald, or for your grandchildren. They look like mighty fine boys."

The mighty fine boys were mighty tired boys at the day's end. As he popped into bed that night, Jack wiggled his toes underneath the cool sheets and breathed a happy sigh.

The evening had been just as exciting as the earlier events of the day. The whole sky over Boston had been aglow with red, green, and purple clouds. Out of the inky blackness, a series of patriotic images had lit up the night.

The boys saw Valley Forge with its snow, bonfires, and stacked muskets. Angry patriots dumped tea in Boston harbor. A brilliant and sparkling Uncle Sam rode in a car with revolving wheels, and the airplane display even had a pinwheel whirling around for a propeller.

At the very end, of course, there was the American flag with the Stars and Stripes appearing in full and glowing color. A barrage of bombs exploded in little bursts of light, echoing through the darkness, and the Fourth of July was over.

Rubbing his eyes sleepily, Jack yawned and murmured into his pillow, "What a great day! It had everything—a parade, a ball game, fireworks, and Grandpa!"

"Midnight Ride of Paul Revere"

ALL THAT week following the Fourth of July a heat wave hung over Boston. Even at the near-by seashore in Hull, where the Kennedy family was spending the summer, the days were sticky and hot, the nights sweltering.

The July sun made the streets a broiling oven as the family drove through the sultry city on the way to Concord one day. When they finally reached the open country, a slight breeze fluttered the leaves and stirred the air.

In the elm-shaded streets of Concord town, the sunlight filtered through the foliage, making cool shadows on the green velvet grass.

"Wish we could take off our shoes and run barefoot," Jack said. "That grass looks cool."

"If you park the car right here, David," Mrs. Kennedy said to the chauffeur, "we can walk over to the statue of the Minute Man. And," she added to Jack, "I don't see why you can't go barefooted. Just watch for sharp stones."

"And don't leave your shoes somewhere, Jack!" As the oldest boy, Joe Jr. took his responsibilities seriously. "Eunice, get down off that runningboard. You know better than to play on the car. Mother, we really shouldn't bring a four-year-old on an outing like this. Eunice is just too young."

"Four years old is not a bit too young to start learning history. I can remember your Grandpa and Grandma Fitzgerald bringing me out here to Concord when I was younger than Eunice." The memories brought a smile to Mrs. Kennedy's lips. "What wonderful history lessons!"

"Grandpa taught you history?" Jack asked.

"Yes. In a way. Of course, we didn't have any classrooms. Nor any textbooks. We didn't need them. Every famous spot within fifty miles of Boston was our classroom. Instead of opening a book, we just opened the doors to history—Old North Church, Bunker Hill, Faneuil Hall, Plymouth Rock, Lexington——"

"Makes the past seem alive," Joe said.

"Reminds me of a game we play at Dexter." Jack's bare toes wiggled the spongy moss.

"No! No football today. Not in your good clothes." Mrs. Kennedy spoke firmly.

"I didn't say anything about football, Mother. It's just a game we play in history class. One fellow thinks of a slogan or a place or a person. Then the other guy matches up a name."

"What a definition!" Joe Jr. gave a snort of disgust. "Better explain the game with an example or nobody will understand it."

"Well——" Jack thought a moment. "For instance, if you say 'One if by land, two if by sea,' what does that remind you of?"

"Paul Revere's Ride!" Kick said promptly.

"Old North Church and the belfry where they hung the signal lantern," Joe replied.

"Henry Wadsworth Longfellow," Mrs. Kennedy said. As the eyebrows shot up, questioning her answer, she explained her choice. "Longfellow wrote the poem. The one that says:

'Listen, my children, and you shall hear
Of the midnight ride of Paul Revere.' "

"I understand your game now, Jack. Can we use dates, too?" Kick asked.

"Don't see why not as long as they match up to a person or a place."

"OK. What does this date remind you of?" she questioned. "April 19th!"

"That's easy," Rosemary answered happily. "It's Uncle Tom's birthday."

36

Mrs. Kennedy smiled. "You're quite right, Rosemary," she said. "But Uncle Tom was born on Patriot's Day, you know. That's the date Kick wants."

"If Uncle Tom was born on Patriot's Day," Jack said, "no wonder he's a history buff."

"The day he was born, back in 1895, your Grandfather Fitzgerald had to make a Patriot's Day speech in Acton. I think he was running for the United States Congress that year. When he finished his speech, your Grandpa announced the birth of a new baby boy—Thomas Acton," Mrs. Kennedy said.

"The people in Acton must have been pleased to have Grandpa name his son after the town. Why did he do that?" Joe asked.

"Mainly because your Grandmother Fitzgerald was born in Acton. But you know how much your grandfather enjoys history. Acton was important in the American Revolution. The entire powder supply of the Continental Army was stored there. Not only that, but an Acton man led the Minute Men at Concord."

"And here we all are right now in Concord, where the Minute Men fought!" Jack was enjoying every minute of this excursion.

Just ahead of Jack and the others a bridge spanned the Concord River. It was a concrete replica of the famous bridge where the Colonials stopped the British. At the far end of the bridge, the Minute Man greeted them. Standing proud and tall, the soldier was a farmer dressed in homespun and carrying his musket ready at his side. The statue was so real and lifelike that Jack almost expected it to speak, to tell what happened on that day in 1775.

At the base of the statue were carved several lines from "The Concord Hymn," the poem that Ralph Waldo Emerson wrote in memory of the skirmish.

"By the rude bridge that arched the flood,
Their flag to April's breeze unfurled,
Here once the embattled farmers stood,
And fired the shot heard round the world."

Beyond the bridge, the family followed a footpath across the adjoining field to the Old Manse, the home of Emerson. The dark gray house with its gambrel roof had been built before the Revolution by Emerson's grandfather. From an upstairs window, his grandmother had watched the battle on the bridge.

Jack thought of all he had read about the Revolution, about the important people and places. The words were now beginning to take on special meaning for him. The past seemed as real as the present. Miles Standish, Paul Revere, Samuel Adams, John Hancock, Ralph Waldo Emerson weren't just names any more. Not after he had walked the same ground where their feet walked, touched the same bricks, stood in the same house, looked at the same sky, the same sea.

As always when they were interested, the children wanted to stay longer and see more. Both boys wanted to visit Nathaniel Hawthorne's old home, The Wayside. The girls, of course, asked to see Orchard House where Louisa May Alcott wrote *Little Women*. Jack explored Walden Pond and imagined Henry David Thoreau writing there in the quiet woods.

All too soon, twilight began to fall on Concord. Dusk moved down over the village from the low ridge of hills and crept along the ancient stone walls, covering the meadows and fields with a deep purple hue. Night was gathering in the quiet streets. Darkness veiled the monuments in the Square, cloaked the Old North Bridge and the Statue of the Minute Man.

From the meeting house steeple, a bell tolled the hour.

"Time to go," Mrs. Kennedy said with great reluctance.

"Let's come back, Mother. This is a terrific way to learn history," Jack said.

"Of course we'll come back," his mother replied. "Everybody needs to know more about history. If you don't know where you've been, how do you know where you're going? We all need to know more about our country's past."

"Look to history for your past," Joe said. "That's a good slogan. What of the present?"

"For the present, look to newspapers," his mother said. "Good newspapers, of course. And magazines like *Literary Digest*. Both are fine. Responsible, accurate reporters give the best look at the present."

"What about the future?" Jack asked.

"The future?" Mrs. Kennedy smiled, but her tone was serious. "The future is up to you."

This Way to
Christmas

THE SKY was the color of lead, heavy with the threat of snow. The clouds across the Charles River Basin bore the dull afterglow of an early winter sunset.

The trolley car careened along the Avenue, clanging loudly when a stray dog crossed the track, when a pedestrian ventured in front.

Jack rubbed the window pane with his mitten, pressed his nose against the frosty glass, and peered out into the twilight. Copley Square looked dingy in the dusk. The streets and buildings along the Avenue all seemed to be huddled up together, waiting for the storm.

"Snow started yet?" asked his grandfather.

"Not really," Jack replied. "I can see a few flakes circling around the street lights."

"Wouldn't be Christmas Eve if we didn't have snow," Mr. Fitzgerald said. "There's nothing in the wide, wide world quite so beautiful as Beacon Hill after a snowfall."

"Dad wouldn't agree with you, Grandpa. He doesn't like any part of Beacon Hill."

"I expect the people on Beacon Hill trouble your father more than the place itself," his grandfather said. "Your father wasn't exactly happy about your coming with me for the carol singing tonight. But Christmas Eve in Boston wouldn't be complete without caroling on Beacon Hill. It's a great tradition and no child ought to miss it. No grown-up, either."

By the time the boy and his grandfather stepped off the street car, the snow was falling swiftly and silently. The lighted shop windows

44

cast a golden glow over the huge white flakes as they drifted down out of the sky.

A wind from the northeast started to blow. It blew gently at first, but then the sharp air slapped Jack on the cheeks and caught him by the throat.

His grandfather pulled his muffler tight. "That's a brisk air, Jack. Haul your ear muffs down, my boy. Wish I had flaps on my derby."

"It's a good thing the girls didn't come with us if it's going to turn this cold," Jack said. "Kick wanted to hear the carolers, but she stayed home to watch the baby so Nurse could do some last-minute shopping."

"That baby! Now he's had his first birthday, Bobby's quite a boy. Last year when he was born, I wasn't sure whether he was going to be a Christmas present or a treat for Thanksgiving!" Mr. Fitzgerald chuckled heartily.

"It was a Thanksgiving for me, all right," Jack

said. "Just to see another boy in this family made me thankful. Maybe Joe will have somebody else to scrap with besides me."

"A little scuffle now and then doesn't do any harm, Jack. Helps keep you in shape."

"That's what Dad says. And I'm all for having a little scuffle now and then. But I don't like to fight every hour on the hour. I won't have any shape left to keep!"

"By the look of those black and blue marks on your chin, you're not doing too well!"

"Grandpa, I'm always black and blue and where I'm not covered with bruises, I've got bandages!" Jack said in mock despair.

"You must have come out second best this time," his grandfather said sympathetically.

"I always seem to come out second best!" Jack had a rueful grin. "And you know how Dad feels about *anybody* coming in second!"

"Cheer up, Jack!" His grandfather was comforting. "You'll be a winner yet. Just keep on trying. Who knows? When Bobby grows up, maybe he'll be on your side."

The snow was falling steadily now. Miniature drifts of the dry fluffy flakes were piling up along the curbs. The city was serene and hushed under its blanket of white. Footsteps made a slight crunching sound and voices were muted on the still, quiet air.

As they passed the Hotel Touraine, Jack peered in at the huge clock in the lobby. "It's still early, Grandpa. Would you take me by Filenes' so I could see the decorations? One of the boys at Dexter told me they have Three Wise Men that move all the way around the building and they are five stories high!"

"A very good height for a Wise Man. Filenes' is an establishment that knows how to promote the Yuletide season. Lead the way."

All the symbols of Christmas were moving

colorfully through the air around the huge old store. Santa Claus cracked his whip animatedly, and his reindeer pawed the earth through waves of brightening and dimming bulbs.

Mr. Fitzgerald looked at his grandson, whose nose was pressed against the store window.

"Got an eye peeled for that electric train?"

"In a way," Jack said, "but not for me."

"Who else?"

Jack grinned. "Wonder if Dad would like it."

His grandfather chuckled. "I suppose you and Joe are too old for a train!"

Jack nodded. "I'd like a Boy Scout knife."

"But you're not a Boy Scout, not yet."

"I will be as soon as I'm twelve," Jack said.

"That's two years or more to wait. Better pick out something you can use now in 1926. See that Flexible Flyer in the next window? Now there's a beauty of a sled."

Suddenly Mr. Fitzgerald doubled up with

laughter. Jack looked puzzled. Mr. Fitzgerald tried to explain between loud guffaws.

"Every time I see a sled, it reminds me of your father taking Joe Jr. sledding. Little Joe wasn't more than a year old. Somewhere along the way, he fell off the sled."

"Grandpa! That's not funny! Was he hurt?"

"Not a bit. Not a peep out of him. He was all bundled up in a coat and leggings, a thick blanket and a buffalo robe. Now the funny part. Your father didn't know Joe fell off. He went whistling on home with the empty sled."

"Wow!"

"Exactly. Your mother was frantic. So was your father. They dashed out in the snow looking for the baby, trying to retrace your father's footsteps. He couldn't remember where he'd been."

"That didn't make it any easier!"

"No, indeed, but at last they found little Joe plunked in a snowdrift, happy as could be, warm

as toast and not a mark on him. But, for a long time, nobody dared say the word *sled* to your father."

Mr. Fitzgerald roared once more with delight. Jack loved to see his grandfather laugh. The boy stood still, enjoying each chuckle.

Holding his sides, Grandpa Fitz gasped for breath. "Jack, we'd best be on our way to Beacon Hill, or we'll miss the carols."

The atmosphere was festive and gay when they climbed up Mt. Vernon Street and reached Louisburg Square. Candlelight glowed from every window of every house. The snow was drifted high against the fence of the little oval park. The statue of Columbus wore a wreath of white snowflakes.

On the steps of a bow-front house in the Square stood a group of Bell Ringers. Men and women, old and young, held one bell in each hand. They rang to and fro as they sang. Perfect in their exacting art, the Bell Ringers could render any Christmas carol or hymn.

"God Rest Ye Merry, Gentlemen" rang out over the cobblestoned streets. "Silent Night, Holy Night" echoed softly on the air. The carolers sang all the old familiar tunes, heartily and reverently, with their audience often joining them in the chorus.

When the director of the Bell Ringers asked if anyone had a request, a little girl standing near Jack spoke up shyly.

"Could you sing the *real* Christmas song?"

"And what might that be, child?"

" 'Happy Birthday,' " the little girl said.

There was a gentle wave of laughter and the director smiled. " 'Happy Birthday?' Aren't you a little mixed up, my dear?"

The little girl shook her head stubbornly. She began to sing in a high, sweet voice, "Happy birthday to you——"

No one said a word and the laughter ceased. There was no need to hurt the youngster's feelings. What if she was a bit confused?

"Happy birthday to you—" she began.

Suddenly the candlelit Square was filled with another kind of glow. As the beauty of the words the child was singing came through to the people standing there, everyone knew it wasn't the *child* who was confused.

"Happy birthday, dear Jesus,
  Happy birthday to you."

For a moment, no one could speak. That whole crowded Square was hushed and silent.

The director leaned down to the upturned face of the little girl. He said gently, "That *was* the real Christmas song. Thank you."

Now other bells began to peal, a lovely sound heard over the voices of the carolers. People began streaming toward the Church of the Advent. The bells rang out, welcoming everyone.

"When you are a little older, I'll take you to a midnight Mass on Christmas Eve. It's like a pageant with wonderful music. But midnight is too late for a growing boy. Too bad the service at the French church is at midnight, too."

"Mother could understand the French service," Jack said proudly.

"She ought to be able to, after studying all those years in Europe!" Grandpa Fitz took his watch out of his vest pocket. As always, he shook his head, then the watch. "Can't put any faith in my time-piece."

"Doesn't it run, Grandpa?"

"Oh, it runs all right. But nobody can catch up with it!" Grandfather Fitz laughed uproariously at his joke, and Jack watched him with pure delight.

"It's time for us to go home, Jack," his grandfather said reluctantly. "Your mother is expecting me to go to church with her."

"Is Mother going to church this late?"

"She always goes on Christmas Eve, Jack. You know how your mother feels about church. She believes it's meant for every day of the week, not just for Sunday. And she's right!"

The big old-fashioned house on Naples Road looked warm and comfortable under the new-fallen snow. Smoke was feathering from the chimneys, and as Jack and his grandfather walked up on the porch they could hear the gay sound of laughter and caroling.

"Your mother must have her own carol service right here. Let's join it," Grandpa said.

Mrs. Kennedy was at the piano with all the family gathered around. The notes of "Adeste Fideles" filled the room. High, sweet, and clear were the voices. "Oh, come all ye faithful," they sang. Jack's reedy young voice joined in with his grandfather's rich baritone.

As the last notes of the chorus sounded, Mr.

Kennedy said, "We used to sing that at the Boston Latin School when I was a kid. And in Latin, too. That song always makes me feel the real spirit of Christmas."

Mrs. Kennedy agreed. "'Adeste Fideles' is the spirit of Christmas in music. What best brings out Christmas in words?"

"The Gospel from St. Luke," Joe Jr. said.

"Dickens' *Christmas Carol*," Kick replied.

"I never thought about it," Jack said.

"There was a message about Christmas from President Coolidge in the paper tonight," Mrs. Kennedy remarked. "He said what we all feel, I think."

"Why not read it to us, Jack? Reading aloud is good practice." His father settled down comfortably in a big leather chair.

Jack picked up the paper, found his place, and read slowly, understandingly. "Christmas is not a time or a season, but a state of mind. To cherish peace and good will, to be plenteous in mercy is to have the real spirit of Christmas. If we think on these things, there will be born in us a Saviour and over us will shine a star sending its gleam of hope to the world."

"Well done, Jack. And well done, President Coolidge. I didn't think the Sphinx of the Potomac had it in him to be so articulate. What paper was that in?" Mr. Kennedy asked.

"The *Boston Evening Transcript*."

Mr. Kennedy bolted up in his chair. The relaxed mellow look fled from his face. "The *Transcript*! I don't want that paper in our house!" He frowned and clenched his fist.

"Why, Dad? What's the matter with it?"

"Everything!" Mr. Kennedy exploded. "I don't think there's anything good about a newspaper that prints the Irish news on a separate page. I'm tired of being called an Irishman!"

"But why? Grandpa Fitz was the first Irish

Mayor that Boston ever had. That ought to make us proud to be called Irish!" Joe Jr. said.

"I don't want to be called an Irishman," his father repeated angrily. "I'll tell you why. I'd like to be called an *American*. My father was born here in America. I was born here. What more do I have to do to be an American?"

"Let's talk about it later," Mrs. Kennedy urged, "after the children are in bed."

"It's the children I'm thinking of!" He choked with his emotion. "I've said it before and I'll say it again. Boston is no place to bring up Irish Catholic children. Maybe times will change someday. But there isn't any sign of it yet. I don't want my children to go through what I went through. We ought to get away from here. This place suffocates me."

Rose Kennedy had been brought up in Boston, too. Her family and friends were all in this city which her husband disliked so much. She loved

Boston as anyone loves a happy home and the places filled with pleasant memories of childhood and family.

Naturally reluctant to leave these familiar scenes for a strange new life in New York, Mrs. Kennedy still put the happiness of the family before her own desires. The Kennedy business operations were centered in New York and Hollywood. Her husband's intense feeling about Boston had reached an extreme. If the move to New York could insure a closer family life, with the children seeing their father regularly and normally, she knew such an undertaking would be right.

Disturbed, but not wanting to disturb the children, she said cheerfully, "Bedtime now. Give your father a good-night kiss. We're all so glad to have him home."

Jack said, "We miss you when you're away, Dad, and you're away so much."

"I miss you, Jack. I miss all of you," Mr. Kennedy said quietly.

"Perhaps—" and Mrs. Kennedy took a deep, deep breath—"perhaps it's time to think seriously about moving to New York." As she saw her husband's delighted smile, she said gently, "But let's not act too hastily. The children should finish their school year here in Brookline. The next six months will give time to find the right place, the right schools."

To Joseph Kennedy, the idea of finally moving to New York was like a huge Christmas package marked especially for him. His frown disappeared completely, his face was wreathed in smiles. Gay and light-hearted, he said, "I'm beginning to think maybe there's a Santa Claus for me, too. Off to bed with you children. When you wake up in the morning, it'll be Christmas." He pointed happily up the stairs. "This way to Christmas, everybody!"

Irish Eyes Are Smiling

As THE train pulled out of Back Bay Station, the iron wheels seemed to have a special kind of rhythm. Clickety-clack. Clickety-clack. The words that went with the tune were special, too, for each member of the Kennedy family.

For Rose Kennedy, the clickety-clack was a slow dirge that seemed to say: "I want to go back! Clickety-clack. Back! Go Back!"

Her eyes misted as she thought of leaving the Boston she loved, of her father and mother and the friends of a lifetime, of the church where she had worshipped daily for so long. But when her vision cleared and she saw the happiness reflected in her husband's face, she did not even question the rightness of the move to New York.

To Joseph Kennedy, those same wheels sang a different song, a gay and cheerful tune.

"Clickety-clack. We'll *never* go back!"

He looked proudly at his family. At long last, they were leaving Boston. To the rising young millionaire, Boston had always been a frustrating wall which he could not break down or jump over.

Neither his wealth nor his powerful political connections had been enough to open any of the doors behind which Beacon Hill and Back Bay Bostonians protected themselves from the Irish. Joseph Kennedy had the same Harvard degree that had been conferred on the sons of old Boston families. Like many Bostonians, he, too, had a beautiful and charming wife, a delightful family. His personal fortune was tremendous.

Yet, because he was the grandson of an Irish

immigrant, the Boston doors which he had hoped to enter remained closed to him, closed to his family. Small wonder he called Boston the city of the broad A and the narrow mind!

His own father, Patrick Kennedy, had known poverty and discrimination. From him Joseph Kennedy had inherited a burning desire to explode the picture of the Irish as servants or clowns. Early in his business career, he had recognized two assets as powerful—a family fortune and a family tree. He planned to give his children both! Purposefully, he set out to acquire in one generation the kind of fortune and cultivated background that had taken centuries for the old Boston families to build.

By the fall of 1927, Joseph Kennedy was well on his way to obtaining the fortune. Moving the family to New York, away from Boston's discrimination against the Irish, was another part of his dream, of his plan.

The large family of Kennedys almost filled the
entire Pullman car. Looking at the gay, happy
faces of the youngsters, Mr. Kennedy said jok-
ingly, "We should have chartered a private car,
Rose. Guess that would have impressed those

stuffy Bostonians." Then he shook his head. "No, and there's the rub. They wouldn't even have noticed! They just ignore what they don't accept! But it won't be like this for our children. Not if I can help it. One of these days, when Joe Jr. is President of the United States, *all* the Irish eyes will be smiling!"

For that matter, his own eyes were smiling now, as he watched the children. Joe Jr. was arguing with Jack, as usual. This time the boys were heatedly discussing the best way to catch a fast pass.

"Who do you think you are? Red Grange?"

"Nope," Jack replied calmly. "But I think I can catch anything you can throw."

"I'll take you up on that. When we get to the new house in Riverdale, first thing—let's see you snag five passes in a row!"

"You're on," Jack said. "First thing."

"First thing!" Joe repeated.

Mrs. Kennedy sighed softly. "They are always arguing. *Always.*"

"I wouldn't worry about it," Mr. Kennedy said. "If you notice, the minute anybody from outside the family picks on either one, they join up forces immediately!"

Across the aisle, Kick was holding little Bobby on her knees, bouncing him up and down and chanting an old tune:

> "See saw, scaradown,
>   Which is the way to Boston town,
>   One foot up, the other foot down,
>   That's the way to Boston town."

Mrs. Kennedy smiled. "I can remember my mother dancing me on her knee to that rhyme when I was a child. There's more to the verse, Kick. It goes:

> "Boston Town's changed to a city
>   But I've no time to change my ditty."

Patricia was sitting on Nurse's lap, half asleep, while Eunice and Rosemary seemed to be taking care of each other. Rosemary especially enjoyed younger children, and Eunice was her favorite. There was a difference of several years in their ages, but the two got along well together. Young as she was, Eunice seemed to understand her oldest sister. Now the two of them were busily pointing out the interesting scenes of the New England countryside as the train sped on.

During a slight lull in conversation, Mr. Kennedy asked, "Boys, what would you think if you could go to a movie and not only see it but *hear* it as well?"

"I'd think I was dreaming. Why?" Jack asked.

"There's a new kind of movie coming out. A talkie. Sort of an experiment. It may fizzle," Mr. Kennedy explained.

"You're kidding, Dad!" Joe Jr. said.

"On the contrary," his father replied.

"You mean you can really hear people talk?"

"Yes, Kick. And more. Al Jolson is going to sing in this movie." Mr. Kennedy smiled at the unbelieving expressions on the faces of the children. "It's called the *Jazz Singer*. I'm anxious to have your comments on it."

"*Our* comments?" Jack asked incredulously.

"Now you *are* kidding," Joe Jr. said.

"Far from it, boys. Remember back a few years ago when I first became interested in the movie industry? You kids both thought Red Grange, that football player, might make a hit in the movies. You boys were absolutely right. He may not be any Rudolph Valentino, but everybody likes to see a football hero."

"The big hero this year is Lindbergh," Jack said. "Going to make a movie of him?"

"I don't know, Jack. He doesn't go much for publicity. Of course, we have him on newsreels with our Pathe News. The whole nation is crazy about Lindbergh," Mr. Kennedy agreed.

"The Lone Eagle!" Joe gave a sigh of admiration. "It must be great to fly all alone up in the clouds with nothing around except you and the sky. When I grow up, I'd like to be a flyer, I think."

"Nonsense, Joe!" His father winked at him. "You're going to be President."

Mrs. Kennedy smiled at both of them. "Those are the exact words your father said when you were born, Joe."

"What did you say, Mother?" Jack asked.

"I said, 'Don't rush him!' I still say it."

Kick put Bobby down on the seat beside her and joined the conversation. "Which would you like to be, Joe? President Calvin Coolidge? Or Charles Lindbergh?"

Joe Jr. replied thoughtfully, "I'd really like to be myself—as President or flyer!"

"Mr. Coolidge isn't going to be President any more, so here's Joe's chance," Jack said. "Of course, right now Joe's a little young and a little inexperienced."

"Stop joking, Jack," Kick said, "and tell me why Mr. Coolidge isn't going to be President?"

"Don't you read the paper, Kick? Or listen to the radio? President Coolidge was out fishing in the Black Hills of South Dakota last month and he announced, 'I do not choose to run.'" Jack spoke with authority.

"Who do you think will be the next President, Dad?" Joe asked.

"I don't really know, Joe. Al Smith might have a chance. He's been Governor of New York for four terms. That's always a good stepping stone to the White House." Mr. Kennedy weighed his words as carefully as if he were talking to a world-famous statesman. "But the Republicans may be able to stay in power."

"President or not, I still think it would be great to fly," Joe said. "Lucky Lindy!"

"Lindbergh wasn't lucky!" Their father's voice was very serious now. "Lucky Lindy! Don't you boys believe it. Lindy was all ready for his opportunity. Prepared. Waiting for his chance. Luck! Rubbish! Here's something to remember. 'Luck favors the prepared mind.'"

"Who said that, Dad?" Jack asked.

"Louis Pasteur. Don't ever forget it and don't ever believe in luck. Opportunity? That's something else again. When opportunity knocks, be prepared. Be ready. And the world will call it luck!"

Touch and Go

THE TANG of November was in the air. The maples had shed their leaves, the oaks still flamed red and scarlet. The ground was a carpet of color—orange, crimson, and gold.

Kick was walking slowly across the lawn, idly scuffing through the drifts of fallen leaves. A loud "Kerchoo" sounded just above her. Startled, she looked up. Her frightened scream echoed through the yard.

"Jack! Get down off that flagpole!"

"Can't come down, Kick. I'm trying to break the record." Jack swayed back and forth at the top of the white pole.

72

"Don't *do* that!" His sister gave a little shriek. "What record?"

"The flagpole sitting record, of course."

"Oh, Jack, you're so silly! Who on earth wants to be a flagpole sitter?"

"I do for one. Lots of other people, too! Did you know that Alvin 'Shipwreck' Kelly sat on a flagpole for 23 days and 7 hours? One of these days, Kick, you will pick up the paper and guess what? My picture will be plastered all over the front page."

She giggled. "Guess what! If you fall off that pole, you'll be plastered all over the front walk!"

"That's sisterly affection for you! Where's Joe? I thought he was going to round up a game of football after school."

"Maybe we can have a quick game before dinner," Kick said eagerly. "Can I be on your side, Jack?"

"Joe will probably choose you, Kick. You're

so good at snagging passes. But if he gets you, I'm going to take Eunice. And Bobby, too."

Kick raised her eyebrows. "A three-year-old playing football?"

"Why not? Bobby is a sure thing with the ball. He's so tiny he can almost run between everybody's legs. Nobody knows where he is until we make a touchdown. It's a shame to waste that kid as waterboy. Call him Touch and Go!"

Kick laughed. "How are you going to play Touch and Go from there on the pole?"

"Easy. Perfect spot. Let me show you how to snag a real high pass." Jack gave the flagpole an extra sway and watched the expression on Kick's frightened face with delight.

"Stop, Jack! You scare me so, with all that wriggling back and forth, I forgot to tell you something important. Come down!"

"Can't come down, Kick. What'd you forget?"

"If you won't come down, there's no reason to

tell you," she replied. "But Margaret baked a chocolate pie with whipped cream."

Whoosh! Jack slid down the pole so fast he ripped his knickers. Holding the seat of his pants, he rushed toward the kitchen.

"Jack!" Kick called after him. "What about the flagpole sitting record?"

"What about it?" He laughed over his shoulder. "There's not a flagpole sitter in the country—not even Alvin 'Shipwreck' Kelly—who wouldn't come down off his perch to taste one of Margaret's pies!"

Later that evening, Jack was twirling the dials of the radio trying to get Graham McNamee's sportscast. Loud squawking and a shrill whistling seemed to be the only entertainment.

"I used to be able to work the radio better when we had that old loudspeaker set," Jack said impatiently. "At least you could put earphones on with that outfit!"

"Progress, Jack, progress!" Joe Jr. said without looking up from his papers.

"It isn't progress if it doesn't work," Jack retorted and turned back to the dials.

Squeak! Squawk! Once he caught the unmistakable tones of H. V. Kaltenborn. Squawk! Amos and Andy tuned in faintly, then faded away. Squeak! The sportscast seemed to be completely off the air. Squawk!

"Stop fiddling with that radio, Jack," Joe spoke sharply. "Can't you see I'm trying to do my homework?"

"I'm not fiddling with the radio. I'm trying to tune in the sports. And you're supposed to do your homework in the library." Jack's tone was as sharp as his brother's.

"Watch it!" Joe doubled up his fist and took a menacing step toward his young brother. "Better not use that bossy tone!"

"Look who's talking!" Jack didn't budge.

Joe Jr. took another threatening step. "You're just asking for trouble, Jack."

The younger boy held his ground. "I'm not afraid of trouble, Joe. You know that!"

"Want to fight?" Joe asked belligerently.

"No, I don't *want* to fight. I'd rather get along with people than fight them, and that goes for you, too, Joe. But, if there's a reason to fight, I'll fight," Jack said.

Jack's attitude seemed to pacify Joe. "To tell the truth, Jack, I really don't want to fight either. I was just cross, I guess. Everybody in the house is cross today. Have you noticed? Even Margaret!"

"I can't imagine Margaret being cross," Jack said. "It doesn't spoil her cooking, that's for sure. She made her best chocolate pie today. What's bothering Margaret?"

"She's all upset over the election results," Joe explained. "She voted for Al Smith."

"So did Dad. But I guess a lot of Democrats must have voted for Hoover," Jack said thoughtfully. "I wonder why, Joe?"

"Everybody has his own answer to that one," Joe replied. "But I guess radio really had a lot to do with Mr. Hoover winning the election. Not because he sounded so good, but because Al Smith sounded so bad! Dad says it's a shame Al Smith wasn't judged on his record. He's been a good Governor for New York, one of the best the state has had."

"How come you're so interested in the election?" Jack asked curiously.

"How could anybody with two ears and two eyes help being interested in politics in *this* family?" Joe answered with a laugh.

"You're so right. The first thing I can remember as a little boy is Grandpa Fitzgerald campaigning for Governor of Massachusetts. I can still hear him singing 'Sweet Adeline'! He doffed his hat to all the ladies, kissed all the babies, and slapped the men on the back."

"Too bad Grandpa didn't win," Joe said. "It would be fun to have a governor in the family."

"Cheer up, Joe. If Dad's dreams come true, we'll all be related to a President."

"What do you mean by that, Jack?"

"You may think Dad is fooling when he says you are going to be President someday. He's dead serious, Joe."

"Oh, I suppose every father would like to have his son be President. I might lose, Jack, if I came up against the same prejudice that Al Smith did in this last election. I think this religious thing can be bad."

"By the time you are grown up, Joe, there probably won't be this feeling about religion," Jack said thoughtfully.

"Do you suppose there will ever be a Roman Catholic in the White House?" Joe asked.

"Already has been," Jack said. "And the roof didn't fall in, either."

"What are you talking about? You know there has never been a Catholic President."

"No, but there was a President who had a Roman Catholic wife. President Tyler."

Joe was astonished. "You're a walking encyclopedia, Jack. Where do you learn it all?"

"Simple. I read books." Jack looked smug.

"OK. So you're a bookworm," Joe said.

"Take that back!" This time, Jack was the one who doubled up his fists.

"OK. I take it back." But Joe chuckled.

"And what's so funny?" Jack asked warily.

"I still think you are!"

"Are what?" Jack was cautious.

"A bookworm!"

As he left the room, Joe dodged the pillow Jack threw at him.

If Jack Kennedy was a bookworm, he knew he

was in good company. The men of history he most liked to read about had been bookworms—Washington, Franklin, Jefferson, Lincoln, Wilson, the two Roosevelts.

He found the life of Teddy Roosevelt especially interesting. As a child, Teddy had been frail and plagued by ill health just as Jack himself had always been.

Just as Teddy Roosevelt's father tried to build up his son's weak body by installing a gymnasium, so Joseph P. Kennedy arranged for athletic instruction so that his children would be in top physical form. Swimming, sailing, horseback riding, golf, tennis, all sports known to man and boy—or to a girl—were played by the Kennedys.

"So I'm a bookworm," Jack thought to himself with a grin. "Maybe it's the early bookworm that gets the bird! Now there's a pun for Grandpa. I can hear him chortle now!"

Tenderfoot at West Point

HIGH ABOVE the Hudson, the ancient ramparts of West Point are always an impressive sight. One John Fitzgerald Kennedy, Tenderfoot Scout in Bronxville's Troop Number Two, looked about him in delighted awe. For a boy who loved history, West Point was Utopia!

Here on these heights, George Washington had supervised the construction of Fort Putnam. The ruins of the Revolutionary fortifications were still standing.

Jack Kennedy stood on the site of the ancient fortress and tried to imagine what it might have been like to be a soldier in the Continental Army.

He could almost hear the clank of the great iron chain as it was laid across the Hudson River from West Point to Constitution Island. Forged by hand, the huge iron links were meant to keep the British warships from sailing up the Hudson, and going north to Fort Ticonderoga and Champlain.

In his mind's eye, Jack could see Benedict Arnold plotting to surrender West Point to the British. How, he wondered, could General Arnold have been such a hero at Saratoga, then a traitor at West Point?

Here on these same fortifications, the United States Military Academy had been started after the Revolution. Ever since 1802, the officers and gentlemen of West Point had served their country in peace and in war.

Jack counted off the wars on his fingers—the War of 1812, the Mexican War, the War between the States, the Spanish-American War, World War I. He remembered all the unsung heroes of the Indian Wars in the West, of the Seventh Cavalry, of the troops that made the frontier safe for the pioneers.

The men of West Point would never have to fight in another war, Jack thought, for now America was at peace with the world. But, the boy said to himself, every patriotic American ought to visit this historic landmark.

The Cadet motto, "Duty, Honor, Country," reminded Jack of King Arthur and the Knights of the Round Table. The covenant of the knighthood was even a little like the Boy Scout Code. Perhaps the noble King Arthur had influenced Cadets and Scouts alike!

The sunset parade had been a thrilling sight. The stirring music of the Army Band made every boy wish he was marching with the Corps of Cadets. As the Long Gray Line passed in review, the colors dipped while the Stars and Stripes flew high in the sky.

Watching the Cadets march off the parade ground in perfect precision, Jack realized that on these same grounds George Washington had commanded, Robert E. Lee had marched, Ulysses S. Grant had drilled, George Custer had ridden, and "Black Jack" Pershing had studied, taught, and fought. History was part of the very atmosphere, as far as the eye could see, as near as the hand could reach.

The excitement of the Parade over, Jack decided to explore the West Point that had not been part of the official Scout tour. His tentmate joined the "Off Limits" safari.

The two boys sauntered off, past the Library with its odd-looking red brick turrets. Directly in front of them was the huge riding hall. Before they could sneak inside, a crusty old non-com of the 1802nd Regiment directed them back to their tents.

The boys waited until the sergeant turned his

back. They ran stealthily into the shadows by the side of Cullum Hall.

"That's Doubleday Field over there in front of us," Chunky whispered. "It's named for General Abner Doubleday, father of baseball."

"I can take or leave baseball. But football! That's something else. Biff Jones is coaching the Army team this year. Wish we could see *him* instead of all the Cadets," Jack said.

"I really like the Cadets, Jack."

"There's nothing wrong with the Cadets, but there's everything right about Biff Jones. Of course," Jack agreed, "one Cadet I would like to meet is the captain of Army's football team. Red Cagle plays a great game and he even writes about football, too."

"Brawn and brains both?"

"You bet," Jack answered. "There's an article by Red Cagle in this month's *Boys' Life*."

"You mean it?" Chunky asked.

Jack nodded. "It's called 'Playing the Back-field.' By Christian K. Cagle. That's his real name. Sometimes they call him Chris, sometimes Red. If you want to read the article, it's on page 7 of the November issue of *Boys' Life*."

"What a memory you've got, Jack!"

"My memory is great for what I want to remember, but I'm a real mess when it comes to the things my father thinks I ought to know."

"Think we should get back? They may miss us," Chunky said.

"I suppose so," Jack agreed reluctantly. "But as a Tenderfoot who has to do all the dirty work around camp, I'm not in a hurry!"

The two boys ambled across to Fort Clinton, looking up the Hudson and enjoying the magnificent view from Trophy Point. Jack could see boats going up and down the river, port and starboard lights gleaming in the twilight. There were several tugs and tankers on the water, and once a foreign freighter gave a toot of its horn as it headed upriver for Albany.

"What a sight it must have been when sailing ships traveled up the Hudson! And just think, Fulton's steamboat used to pass right by this point." Jack was alive to the beauty and meaning of the past, although no boy could possibly be a more active part of the present.

Around the campfire that night, Jack was strangely silent. The flickering orange light sent eerie shadows racing across the canvas tents. The popping and snapping of the wood added a staccato note to the music of the Scouts' gay songfest. They sang rollicking tunes of the present and the past, hiking songs, and Scout ditties.

As the fire died down to embers that glowed against the dark of the night, the Scoutmaster led the troop in the Scout Oath.

Jack joined with the other boys in repeating

the creed. Once again, he found himself thinking that Boy Scouts were a sort of modern-day
version of King Arthur's noble knights.

"Then all the knights arose and each knight
held up before him the cross of the hilt of his
sword and each knight spake as King Arthur
—" Jack remembered the Covenant of the
Round Table even as he heard himself saying,
"On my honor I will do my best——"

And all the boys' voices rose as one, "—to do
my duty to God and my country and to obey the
Scout law; to help other people at all times, to
keep myself physically strong, mentally awake,
and morally straight."

Sailing Against the Storm

THE OFFSHORE breeze blew gently on the surfless waters, stirring the dunegrass and bending the feathery gray tufts of the beach rushes. This world of the sand dunes held a special kind of enchantment for young Jack Kennedy, a changeless yet always changing background for the Cape Cod he loved.

Motionless though they seemed to be, the dunes were always moving, restless as the sea itself. Nothing grew there but dusty miller, beach pea, bayberry, and poverty grass. The occasional tree was stunted and toughened by the winds and the salt air. Even the scrub pine gave up the struggle with the sands and the sea. Yet there was a beauty in the pale shadows of the shifting sands, in the flowing shapes sculptured by the wind.

In a sheltered cove beyond the dunes, Jack and his sister Kathleen were digging clams, their only companion a grave-faced gull.

Digging clams, Jack Kennedy could tell you, was serious business. Clams—Cape Cod clams, at least—lived exactly nine inches below the surface of the sand and they moved with the speed of lightning. Each time Jack located his target and poked his shovel straight down, sure of success, the clam had shot six feet to the left and was laughing heartily up his shell!

After what seemed eternity, Jack and Kick had acquired a bucket of clams. They had also dug up a cart full of old shoes and discarded bottle caps.

"Is there any legal limit to the number of

bottle caps you can dig up?" Jack asked in a tone of utter disgust.

Kick laughed. "I don't mind the bottle caps. They don't spit at you the way clams do!"

"Let's call a halt to this clammy business and go sailing," Jack suggested. "Join me?"

"Where are you bound?" she asked.

"Nowhere special. Just out for a little bit of salt air." He slipped his bare feet into an ancient pair of sneakers.

"That's forbidden, Jack, and you know it. No one in this family goes sailing without telling where he's bound. Suppose a squall comes up? If you're caught in it, nobody will know where to start looking for you."

"You sound just like Miss Cahill, and I'm too old to have a governess. Remember I'm going away to school in another week. You'll miss me, Kick. Better go sailing with me while you can. The two of us can handle any old squall on

Nantucket Sound." Jack knocked on a piece of driftwood, smiling at Kick as he did so.

"I'll go if you'll name the spot where we'll be headed," Kick insisted stubbornly.

"OK, you win. And you're right of course. If we don't go too far, we'll be back in time to see the new Harold Lloyd movie. It's his first talking film. *Welcome Danger*. Ought to be funny. Where do you want to sail?"

"You name it, Jack, as long as we tell somebody here at the house where we'll be."

"If we took the boat over to Osterville, I could stop a minute and talk with Captain Manley. Dad says if I go to Canterbury and get decent marks all through the school year, he just *might* ask the Crosbys to build me a sailboat—a Wianno!"

Jack wasn't at all anxious to go away to boarding school. He loved the close family life, the give and take of the Kennedy clan. He would

miss the togetherness of the large, happy family. But, anxious or not, Jack was entered at Canterbury School for the fall term and would leave for Connecticut and the New Milford campus in another week.

Later that afternoon, Jack had a man-to-boy talk with H. Manley Crosby, the Captain Manley of Wianno fame.

"You brought that boat into harbor like a real sailor, Jack," Captain Manley said, "almost like a native!"

"We ought to be called natives by now, hadn't we?" Jack asked the elderly gentleman.

"Impossible!" Captain Manley said.

"But why not, sir? We've been coming to Hyannis every summer since I can remember."

"Well," and Captain Manley looked seaward as if in search of some kind way to explain this obvious truth, "it's this way——"

He leaned down on the wharf and picked up a

kitten from the litter nestled there asleep in the warm afternoon sun. "If this mother cat jumped on your stove and had these kittens in the oven, you wouldn't call them biscuits, would you?"

The boy doubled up with laughter. "Wish my Grandfather could have heard that one, Captain Manley. You explained and then some. I wish you could explain to my Dad why I ought to have a Wianno to sail next summer!"

"I could try," Captain Manley said, "but the Wianno explains herself. Whether your Dad wants a family day sailer or a powerful racing boat, this craft fills the bill. Nantucket Sound can be windy and treacherous. The Wianno stands up in these rough waters."

"I figure she can take me any place I dare to go," Jack said. "The keel class doesn't stand much of a chance on the Sound."

"No," Captain Manley agreed. "These shoal waters take a shallow draft."

98

"You designed the Wianno, didn't you, sir?"

"Yes, Jack. I suppose that's why I'm so proud of her. There have been Crosby boats in these waters since 1850, but the first Wianno Senior raced in the summer of 1914, a few years before you were born. Your father will be interested to know that in all these years, a Wianno has never capsized."

"When you build my first Wianno," Jack said, "I'm going to call it 'Victura.' That means something about winning and I like to win."

Kick called up from the boat, "What's keeping you, Jack?"

"Excuse me, sir," Jack said. "Kathleen's impatient to be on our way."

"You youngsters don't want to get too far out in the Sound this late in the afternoon. Those clouds overhead might mean trouble."

Those clouds *did* mean trouble!

The sea that Jack and his sister faced that

September afternoon was not the sea of summer sailing, yacht clubs, catboats, and cabin cruisers. It was the sea of the clipper ships and the whaling vessels. It was the sea of wind-lashed headlands and fierce waters, a place of raging gales and booming surf.

One moment the sky had been tranquil and serene. The next, it had suddenly darkened. The air turned bitter. The wind struck like a hammer. The sea became darkly, threateningly blue, inky in color. The breaking waves looked vicious, bleak, and sullen.

Without warning, a dense fog closed in, hugging the surface of the sea. Gray, thick, and soupy as the fog was, Jack could still see the angry waters below. He knew he should be scared, but there just wasn't time! He had to get the boat and his sister back to safe harbor! He *had* to!

On the shore in Hyannisport, Joe Jr. stood

on the Kennedy dock with his father, peering anxiously out into the expanse of nothing.

Although they both knew Jack was an expert sailor, they also knew that he was only thirteen and his sister barely ten. This was a dangerous fog, a dangerous storm. The fishermen called it a dungeon fog, the dread of all the men who go down to the sea in ships.

Joe Jr. leaned against the wet post of the dock, drenched by the surf. He listened. He waited. Without meaning to, he shivered.

"Of course, they are all right," he said.

His father echoed, "Of course." But his eyes were miserable.

"Jack has brought that boat through worse weather than this," Joe Jr. said with a heartiness that fooled neither of them. "He's brought her in a thousand times!"

"A thousand times," his father repeated, his voice pinched and strained.

The moments passed slowly, dragging into hours. Both father and son were startled by the whistle of the Nantucket steamer. That whistle, low and resonant, could be cheerful on a bright sunny day, or romantic on a moonlit night. But in this dense fog, the sound was sharp and melancholy, like a warning.

Finally, the surf died down. So did the wind. But still the fog did not lift.

Suddenly, out of the grayness came the little sailboat, her bow sheering the water cleanly, heading straight to the dock as if drawn by a taut string.

Kathleen, white-faced and drawn, gave Jack a weak smile before she stepped on the dock.

Jack *seemed* as calm as if he'd been steering through the glories of a flaming sunset.

"Thick out there this afternoon," he said casually as he brushed the hair out of his eyes and staggered wearily toward the house.

102

Canterbury
Tales

THE COMMON ROOM at Canterbury's North House was full of boys doing exactly the same thing, writing a letter home. Jack Kennedy chewed his pencil, looked up at the ceiling.

"Psst," he whispered to the boy sitting next to him. "How do you spell *literary?*"

"L-i-t—" the boy began, "—r-y, I think."

"Are you sure that's right?" Jack asked.

"If you've got to be sure, ask the dictionary, not me. Can't you use another word?"

"Hardly," Jack replied. "Not when I'm asking my Dad to send me the *Literary Digest.*"

Although the school library stocked magazines

and newspapers, Jack wanted to have his own look at current affairs. He missed the talks around the dinner table at home, the give-and-take discussions of the past, the present, and the future.

Laboriously, he kept at his letter. "We are reading *Ivanhoe*," he wrote, "and although I may not be able to remember material things such as gloves, tickets and so forth, I can remember *Ivanhoe* and the last time we had an English exam, I got a 98."

He drummed the table with his pencil, then started to write swiftly. "More good news. I can swim like a fish. Fifty yards in thirty seconds. The swimming coach thinks swimming is very important because it's a sport that can save lives. I never thought of it that way but I guess he is right. Who knows? Someday my being able to swim may save my life. Or better yet, somebody else's!"

The boy frowned. He was duty bound to write about his Latin marks. Perhaps if he tucked his grades in between the swimming item and the 98 in English——

"Mr. Brodie," he wrote, "says I can do better than this in Latin. As a matter of fact, Mr. Brodie thinks *anybody* can do better than this. But Mr. Brodie is a Rhodes Scholar and very bright. He actually *likes* Latin!"

Jack thought a moment, then continued, "He told all of us in his Latin class that most people consider Latin the beginning of a liberal education. Then he sort of smiled and said, 'If you young sprouts don't study Latin, you just won't get into college!' I guess he knew that would get through to us. It did to me."

Young Kennedy sat back in his chair. That last line, he thought, was a stroke of genius. It might convince his father that Jack was studying. The boy shook his head and sighed. His father was not easily convinced, he knew, nor easily fooled.

Purposefully, he wrote, "I'm going to try and get my marks up in Latin. I really mean it this time."

That *would* please his father. For his mother, he wrote, "If I knew more about Latin, I could understand the Latin part of the Mass. I'm getting very pious with chapel so often. I'm also cold at night. Please send up a puff."

The second part of his letter was important to him. At Christmas, just before starting back to Canterbury for the second term, Jack had finally got up courage enough to ask his father for a larger allowance.

Mr. Kennedy had been in the library poring over papers when the boy knocked on the door. Although Jack had prepared a polished speech for the occasion, he forgot it completely when the occasion finally arose.

Fidgeting with the button on his jacket, he blurted out, "Dad, how about a raise?"

Mr. Kennedy leaned back in his chair and looked at Jack over his horn-rimmed glasses. "Well, how about it? I presume you mean a raise in your marks?"

Jack's eyebrows shot up. "Not exactly. I was thinking about a raise in my allowance."

"Hmmmm." Mr. Kennedy appeared to think it over. Was he serious? Or joking? Jack just couldn't tell.

"You think you need a raise in your allowance," Mr. Kennedy went on. "I think you need to raise your marks. Perhaps we can get together. Why don't you put down in writing all the reasons that make you think you deserve a raise?"

Now in Canterbury's Common Room, Jack was doing just that. He had crossed out, written over, and erased. Finally he set his jaw, took another sheet of paper and wrote:

"Plea for a Raise

"My recent allowance is 40¢. This I used for airplanes and other playthings of childhood but now I am a Scout and I put away my childish things. Before I would spend 20¢ of my 40¢ allowance and in 5 minutes, I would have empty pockets and nothing to gain and 20¢ to lose.

"When I am a Scout, I have to buy canteens, haversacks, blankets, searchlights, ponchos— things that will last for years and I can always use it while I can't use chocolate marshmallow ice cream sundaes and so I put in my plea for a raise of 30¢ for me to buy Scout things and pay my own way around."

He read it over, changed a word, sealed the letter quickly and headed for his room.

It was Saturday. For one whole hour in the afternoon, Canterbury boys were allowed to go out on the town. The Village Green swarmed with young men who had saved up their money through the week for a chocolate soda, a candy bar, or a malt.

Eating between meals was strictly forbidden

at Canterbury, and no food was ever allowed in the rooms. These rules and regulations made the Saturday hour in New Milford seem like an oasis in the desert. The sight of the Village Green with its towering elms and maples, its old-fashioned Victorian bandstand, and its corner drugstore was a glimpse of Utopia.

Jack stopped in the room across the hall to borrow a stamp for his letter. A redheaded, freckle-faced boy was sprawled out on the window seat, unhappily watching the motionless frog on the sill.

"What's the matter, Tim? Has Mr. Brodie flunked you in Latin again?"

"Nothing so simple as that," the boy answered. "It's my frog. Frisky just isn't living up to his name any more. He's droopy."

"All frogs are droopy in cold weather," Jack said. "What do you feed him?"

"Oh, all the things you're supposed to feed

frogs. Flies, spiders. I even fed him a fly covered with red pepper," Tim went on. "Didn't pep him up."

"Why don't you set off a firecracker under him?" Jack asked with a chuckle.

"That's not funny," Tim replied. "I already tried it. Frisky didn't even wiggle, but I got two demerits when the housemaster heard all the racket. Think of something else."

"Well, maybe old Frisky's number is up."

"Oh gosh, no!" Tim was horrified.

"Nobody can live forever. Not even frogs."

"I wanted to keep him to show my little brother when I go home for Easter vacation."

"Keep him then," Jack said unsympathetically.

"How can I keep him if he's dead?"

"Easy. The Science Master keeps his frogs in the lab all year long. They look alive but they are stone cold dead. Preserved."

"Jack, maybe you've got something!" Tim was elated. "If you can preserve a dead frog, why can't you preserve a live one? Droopy this frog may be, but he's alive. Just think, Jack, if Frisky could be preserved *before* he dies, then maybe he'd never die!"

Jack looked skeptical. "The science lab is closed for the weekend. You can't preserve him today and he may not last until Monday. If we knew what was in that stuff, we could brew up a batch and toss Frisky into the brine."

"Brine!" Tim said the word and snapped his fingers with glee. "Brine! That's it, Jack! Pickles come in brine. You know the grocery store half-way down the hill? Booth's? We'll preserve Frisky in Booth's pickle barrel. Want to come along, Jack?"

"Sure, but remind me to mail this letter to my Dad on the way. Got an extra stamp? After we plop Frisky into the pickle barrel, we could hike down to the drugstore and get a chocolate marsh-mallow sundae. By the time we're back, Frisky ought to be pretty well pickled."

This is just what Jack and Tim did—or tried to do. Jack stood guard, shielding Tim from sight of the clerk in Booth's store. Tim took Frisky

112

out of his pocket and, when no one was looking, dropped the frog into the pickles.

The boys shook hands gravely.

"Well done, my good man," Tim said, politely.

"Nothing to it, old chap," Jack replied.

He held the door for the stout lady who entered the grocery store just as they were leaving. Then, licking their lips in anticipation, the boys headed down the hill toward the drugstore and their chocolate sundae.

Halfway across the street, they were halted by the bloodcurdling scream that echoed from Booth's. They looked at each other, mystified. With one accord, the two boys dashed back to the store.

They were just in time to hear the stout lady screech, "Those pickles are *alive!*" With a thud and a thump that shook the grocery shelves, she fell to the floor.

Immediately, the place was in an uproar. The

two boys standing in the doorway were strangely silent, but nobody noticed them.

"Somebody *do* something!" a girl screamed.

The clerk leaped from behind the counter, wringing his hands helplessly. "Please!"

"Giv 'er air!" a woman shouted.

"Ladies, please control yourselves," the clerk said, wiping his forehead with his sleeve.

"Water! She needs water."

"Ladies, please!" The clerk was desperate.

"Giv 'er air!" the woman shouted again.

In the midst of all the excitement, the incredible happened. Frisky, the frog, came leaping out of the pickle barrel.

Everyone yelled at once. Tim and Jack edged toward the entrance door.

"Those pickles *are* alive!"

"Ladies, please control yourselves."

"Call the police."

One frantic matron pushed the red button

saying emergency only. There was a loud clang. The old-fashioned burglar alarm went off and the overhead fire sprinkler suddenly started to spray.

The tomcat that was always sunning himself in Booth's window moved quickly for once—too quickly. He scooted between the aisles, tripping two of the frightened customers and knocking over a display of tunafish. A towering pyramid of soup cans swayed precariously, then came tumbling down with a crash. The cans rolled noisily in every direction.

The frog seemed to have more sense than any of the people. Frisky just hopped over by the door. Without even a backward look, Jack and Tim joined their frog friend and walked casually out into the chill February air.

In a few moments, the two boys, a trifle shaken but convulsed with laughter, were on their way back up the hill to Canterbury.

"These pickles are alive," Tim shrieked in a high falsetto.

"Please control yourself!" Jack mimicked the clerk's nervous tones exactly.

"Frisky isn't droopy any more, Jack. He's hopping up and down all over my pocket!"

"Wonder what did it?" Jack was enjoying himself. "Was it the pickling? Or the yelling!"

Turkey Talk

AROUND THE Thanksgiving table, heads were bowed in grace. One pair of eyes was not closed. Jack Kennedy just had to watch over the huge turkey in front of his father's place!

Mr. Kennedy picked up the carving knife. "Who wants a drumstick?"

Nine children had the same answer, from seventeen-year-old Joe Jr. to nine-month-old Teddy. Teddy couldn't speak, but his "da" meant "I do" just as the others' words did.

"Someday," Jack said, his mouth full of turkey, "somebody ought to invent a turkey with at least a dozen legs. Sort of a cross between a turkey and a centipede. Just imagine, Thanksgiving and each one of us with a drumstick!"

"Please don't talk with your mouth full, Jack," Mrs. Kennedy said, "and pass the cranberries."

"Jack, you sound just like Bobby's pig when you eat so fast!" Kick said.

"Don't talk that way about Porky!" Bobby had just celebrated his seventh birthday a few days before and he was feeling his years. "Porky's the best pet I ever had."

"Whoever heard of a pig for a pet?"

"I have, that's who!" Bobby was on the defensive. "Porky's my best pet."

"Quit this Porky talk!" Jack warned, "or we'll all wind up speaking pig Latin!"

"Never mind the pig Latin," Mr. Kennedy said. "How's your real Latin shaping up, Jack?"

The boy shifted uneasily. "Well, now that Mr. Morgan is teaching me, I'm passing. He says I *could* be a good Latin student."

"That's not what I asked you, Jack. I know you *could* be a good Latin student. You *could* be a good student in every class at Choate. But, this doesn't mean you *are!*" His father looked at him sharply. "What Mr. Morgan thinks you *could* do in Latin, what Mr. Packard figures you *ought* to do in French, what Russ Ayres and Mr. Hemenway think you *should* be getting in history—none of this matters unless *you* do something about it yourself!"

Joe Jr. spoke up. "Cappy Leinbach says Jack can do well in anything he really wants to do."

"Who is Cappy Leinbach?" Rosemary asked.

"Rosemary! That's sacrilege! Cappy Leinbach is one of the most important people at Choate! To me, anyhow. He's the best football coach in the Junior League. Teaches algebra," Jack said.

"Why does he know so much about you?"

"He was a housemaster at Choate House last year while Jack roomed there," Joe Jr. said.

"Not only that, but my bedroom was right next to the Leinbachs' living room," Jack added with a grin. "We used to have some terrific bull sessions. I'll never forget them. Used to have some terrific waffle sessions, too, and I won't forget those, either. The Choate catalog ought to list Mrs. Leinbach's Sunday night waffles as an extracurricular activity."

"Bet you didn't get away with much, not if you roomed right next to the master," Kick said.

"Nope," Jack said as he reached for another slice of turkey, "but I tried."

"Haven't stopped trying, have you?" His father looked at Jack over his horn-rimmed glasses. "Mr. Maher writes you were caught going out over the windowsill after lights out. I don't like that sort of letter from a housemaster."

Jack flushed. "It seemed like a terrific idea at the time. Lem Billings and I went down the Hill

120

to O. D. Footes' for a chocolate marshmallow sundae. Nobody gets away with anything at Choate!"

"A lot of them try," Joe Jr. said. "A fifth-former was expelled for smoking last week."

"That no-smoking rule is a good thing," Mr. Kennedy said firmly. "I'll make a bargain with each one of you. If you won't smoke or drink until you are twenty-one, I'll write out a check for $1000 and hand it over to you on your twenty-first birthday. If you've kept the bargain, you can keep the check. But I'll expect it back if you've ever smoked or had a drink."

"That's only six years for me to wait," Jack said, "But poor Teddy here will have to stick around for twenty-one more years."

"Cappy Leinbach may have taught you algebra, Jack, but you still can't count," Joe said. "Teddy was born in February, remember?"

"How could anybody forget a brother born on

Washington's birthday? Who knows? Maybe Ted will grow up to be President."

"That's Joe's job," Mr. Kennedy said. "Joe is going to be President."

Jack grinned. "If Joe's going to be President, he may have to hire a cigarette holder even if he doesn't smoke. That cigarette holder of Franklin D. Roosevelt's is a trademark."

"I don't care who smokes," Kick said. "It's a silly, smelly habit."

"Off with your head, Kick. You're talking about our newly elected President," Jack said.

"Isn't Mr. Hoover President?" Pat asked.

"Herbert Hoover *is* President, Pat, but only until March fourth. Then Mr. Roosevelt will be inaugurated," Mr. Kennedy explained. "First Democrat in twenty years! This makes your Grandfather Fitzgerald happy, but I wish Grandpa Kennedy could have lived to see this day. He was afraid America would never get a

Democrat in the White House again. I was beginning to have the same fear."

"Did you hear the election returns, Dad?"

"Of course, Joe," Mr. Kennedy replied. "Don't forget I campaigned for F.D.R. How about you boys? Did you listen at school?"

Both boys spoke at the same time. "No sir," Joe Jr. said. "Yes, sir," Jack said.

Mr. Kennedy looked sharply at the two of them. "You said no, Joe! Why not? That's a peculiar lack of interest for a fellow who might be President someday!"

"It wasn't that, Dad. Radios aren't allowed in dorms at Choate," Joe Jr. explained.

"Hmmm." Mr. Kennedy turned toward Jack. The boy was squirming uncomfortably. "You said yes, Jack. How did you hear the returns?"

"Well, I—uh—used to listen to the radio at the Leinbach's last year. I still drop by to see them and, once in a while, I listen to the radio.

Besides, Mr. Hemenway asked us to listen to the Presidential campaign speeches. He says history isn't just a study of the past. It's knowledge of the present. Someday, I bet Mr. Hemenway will start a regular course in public affairs. We even ran a mock election."

"Who won?" Kick asked.

"Who won? At Choate? Don't ask silly questions! It was a Hoover landslide," Jack said. "But don't worry, Dad. I voted for F.D.R."

Mrs. Kennedy's voice sounded slightly troubled as she asked, "Academics and athletics are important, but so is your faith. Are you sure you're being true to your Church, Jack?"

"Mother, I'm down in Wallingford at Holy Trinity every Sunday morning!"

"Good for you! But remember, religion isn't just for Sunday. It should be a part of every day." She added, "And not just for Jack, but for each one of us."

Choate Charts the Course

WHEN HIS Choate School classmates voted him "Most Likely to Succeed," Jack Kennedy thought the boys in his graduating class were joking. So did everyone else, including his teachers and his family. In both academics and athletics, Jack had always played second fiddle to his dynamic older brother, Joe Jr.

Yet the experiences of this period influenced all of his life. The friendships made during these years were of lifelong duration. A world of ideas was discovered, and a world of ideals was revealed. Young Jack Kennedy began to grow up at Choate.

In his senior year, he finally wrote to his father, "Dad, I've definitely decided to stop fooling around."

His father's reply was prompt and encouraging. "Now, Jack, I don't want to give the impression that I'm a nagger for goodness knows that is the worst thing any parent can be. After long experience in sizing up people, I definitely know you have the goods and can go a long way. Now aren't you foolish not to get all there is out of what God has given you? After all, I would be lacking even as a friend if I did not urge you to take advantage of the qualities you have."

The school yearbook, *The Brief,* also reported that Jack Kennedy, like his father and older brother Joe Jr., would enter Harvard in the fall of 1935. But where *The Brief* was correct in prophesying Jack's ability to succeed, the yearbook was wrong in predicting the college he would attend.

Jack enrolled at Princeton with Lem Billings, his roommate at Choate. Although Mr. Kennedy found it hard to believe that Jack could prefer any institution to Harvard, he was both amazed and pleased at his son's show of independence. Jack was amazed and pleased himself!

His father did insist, however, that Jack spend the summer studying at the London School of Economics as Joe Jr. had previously done. Unfortunately, Jack had barely enrolled when he fell ill with jaundice and was forced to return home from London. He regained his health in the sun and sand of Hyannisport and entered the fall session at Old Nassau. Billings was once more his roommate.

A return attack of jaundice interrupted the freshman year at Princeton. Much as Teddy Roosevelt went West to build up his frail body several decades before, so Jack Kennedy went to Arizona and worked on a ranch to recuperate.

The following fall, he bowed to his father's wishes and entered Harvard. A familiar pattern repeated itself. Jack found himself running a poor second to Joe Jr. At Harvard, his brother was the Big Man on Campus—a varsity football player, a leading campus politician, and a superior student.

Jack, on the other hand, was never able to make the varsity in any sport. However, he did play on the junior varsity football team until he injured his spine in a scrimmage. He also earned a place on the Harvard swimming team. In his second year, he won a spot for himself on the business board of the "Harvard Crimson," but in college politics, he was always a loser.

However, national politics was of vital interest to the whole Kennedy family. Joseph Kennedy, one of the chief Roosevelt supporters in 1932, backed F.D.R. again in 1936. Roosevelt campaigned successfully against Governor Alfred Landon of Kansas. "Life, Liberty, and Landon" was the Republican slogan, but the American voters put the New Deal back in operation.

It was late in 1937 that President Roosevelt announced the appointment of the new Ambassador to the Court of St. James, Joseph P. Kennedy. Bostonians were not the only ones to be stunned by Roosevelt's choice. To send an Irish Catholic to London astonished everyone! But Joseph Kennedy and his gracious wife dazzled all of Britain. The large family of handsome boys and girls was an exciting addition to the staid diplomatic circles.

Summer vacations from college were spent traveling in Europe or at the Embassy in London. The Kennedys also rented a villa on the French Riviera.

During the Junior year at Harvard, Jack was allowed a leave of absence to study international relations firsthand. Young Kennedy observed the turmoil of Europe with his mind as well as with his eyes. He asked opinions, made comparisons, came to conclusions. The carefree school boy began to disappear. In his place developed the man who would one day represent the people of America.

When Jack returned to Harvard, he showed a marked maturity of thought. His thesis in political science showed such understanding of international affairs that he was urged to expand the paper into a book. *Why England Slept* was a best seller and considered a remarkable work for so young an author.

In June of 1940, John F. Kennedy graduated from Harvard with honors in political science. Not even the *cum laude* on his diploma made him as happy as a cable from Ambassador Kennedy: "Two things I always knew about you. One— that you are smart. Two—you're a swell guy."

That spring of Jack Kennedy's graduation marked a black-bordered year for Europe. The German Nazis staged their first great offensive after Poland. Denmark, Norway, the Netherlands, and Belgium collapsed under the *Blitzkrieg*. Hitler's troops outflanked the supposedly impregnable Maginot line and swept on over France.

The continent of Europe was in Nazi hands as the British forces prepared to evacuate Dunkirk. The curtain of history rose on World War II.

A Skipper for Uncle Sam

"SORRY!" The Air Corps flight surgeon said the back injury Jack Kennedy had suffered while playing JV football disqualified him.

"Sorry!" The Army doctors turned him down. His back could not stand combat strain.

"Sorry!" The Navy physicians said. "It's that bad back of yours."

Unlike Joe, who was winning his wings as a Navy pilot, Jack had a struggle to get into uniform. Although America was officially at peace, the summer of 1941 found the nation on the brink of the war that was raging in Europe. Jack wanted to be a part of whatever might happen.

In a desperate effort to strengthen his back, he put himself through a program of rigorous exercises. After five months of daily dozens, he was declared fit for the Navy. Proudly, he donned the blue uniform, but he was disappointed at being assigned a desk job in the Pentagon. He pulled every string to win a combat assignment. After Pearl Harbor, he hounded everyone in the hope of getting sea duty.

He finally realized his ambition when he was sent to Patrol Torpedo Boat School in Rhode Island. For six months, Jack learned how to handle the dangerous PT boats. His years of sailing on the waters of Nantucket Sound were now a boon. He was considered "an old salt."

Early in 1943, his address become APO, San Francisco. The vast air, sea, and ground attack that was taking shape in the South Pacific included Jack Kennedy, Skipper of PT 109.

To her young and enthusiastic skipper, this

PT boat was something more than special. Riding her at high speed was an exhilarating bout with wind and spray. In choppy seas she slapped the water so hard that a sailor had to keep his balance by the spring of his knees, like a skier on a bumpy slope.

PT 109 saw hard and dangerous service. By August, 1943, she had completed thirty successful missions and her crew almost believed she was indestructible.

The thirty-first mission was different.

That night PT 109 was patrolling the dark waters off the Solomon Islands. Skipper Kennedy was at the wheel, and all hands were at their stations, their eyes straining to see any Japanese target.

Suddenly the lookout yelled, "Ship at two o'clock!" and out of the inky darkness loomed the towering shape of an enemy destroyer. Before anyone could move, the destroyer struck

135

the 109 like a charging skyscraper and rushed on through the night.

The wheel was torn from Kennedy's grasp and he was flung against the deck, flat on his back. With a violent wrench, the boat broke in two. Orange flames exploded in the engine room, knocking "Pappy" McMahon, the engineer, against a bulkhead. Flames of the high octane gasoline scorched his body and spilled over the waters. His half of the boat quickly sank and he fought his way back to the surface, only to find himself in a sea of fire.

The gasoline was still burning on the water as Kennedy struggled to his feet. His half of the 77-foot hull stayed afloat. Three of the crew were still aboard. The able swimmers dived into the water searching for survivors.

In a few moments Jack found McMahon. He was in agony, his hands, arms, and face seared black by the flames.

"Skipper, I'm done for," McMahon gasped.

"Stick with me, Pappy," Kennedy said, and gently towed the suffering seaman to the boat.

Harris, the Gunner's Mate, had an injured leg. "I can't swim, Skipper."

"Try, Harris," Kennedy urged.

"I can't," Harris cried. "I can't make it."

"For a man from Boston, Harris, you're certainly putting up a great exhibition out here!" Jack said in a matter-of-fact tone. He guided Harris safely back to the wreck.

Dawn was rising in the east before the men gave up hope of finding the two missing crewmen. Then, examining the wreckage, they discovered that the first aid kit was gone and there was no food except for a box of salt water taffy. The only weapons they had were two knives and Kennedy's sidearms. They were in shark-infested waters, surrounded by Japs.

"We're not exactly shipshape," Jack said,

"but we're alive." He went on to discuss their plight. "There's nothing in the book about this. A lot of you have wives and children. What do you want to do? I have nothing to lose."

The men decided unanimously against surrender. They chose to swim to a coral island three miles away. This island was too small to be occupied by the Japs. They prepared for the long haul by using a timber from the boat for a raft. Clinging to the timber, they pushed it along toward the island by kicking their feet.

McMahon could not hold on the raft with his burned hands, but he could float in a life jacket. Tying the straps of the jacket together, Kennedy took the straps in his teeth. "I'll tow Pappy," he said and started to swim toward the island, towing McMahon behind him.

The sun was low in the afternoon sky when Kennedy heard the sound of waves on the reef and knew they had reached the island at last.

By this time he had been swimming for more than five hours.

"Pappy," Kennedy said weakly, "we're in!"

All the world knows the grim story of the crew's fight to stay alive, of their Skipper's long swim for help, of the eventual rescue.

Jack Kennedy had almost given up hope, but when the boat arrived to take the crew back to base, his wry sense of humor sprang to life.

"Where have you been?" he asked lazily.

"Hey, Jack!" the skipper of the rescue boat shouted. "We've got some food for you."

"No, thanks," Jack said. "Just had a coconut!"

The journey back to Rendova was as hilarious a mission as the United States Navy ever undertook in the South Pacific. The two Gizo natives who rescued the crew had attended mission schools before the war. They had learned one song, which they sang over and over again.

The waters of the Solomons echoed and re-echoed with the rousing refrain: "Jesus loves me, this I know, for the Bible tells me so——"

The Navy awarded John F. Kennedy the Purple Heart and the Navy and Marine Corps Medal. Admiral William F. Halsey signed the citation which said 'in part, "His courage, endurance, and excellent leadership contributed to the saving of several lives and was in keeping with the highest traditions of the United States Navy."

Rotated home from the South Pacific, Jack was hospitalized for malaria and spinal surgery. He was still in the Navy hospital, recuperating, when his parents received a telegram from the War Department. Joe Jr. had been killed in action over Europe.

The whole Kennedy family was plunged into deepest gloom. Jack's own grief took tangible form in a privately published book of tribute to his brother, *As We Remember Joe.*

The words of family and friends were eloquent, but none were more touching than Jack's own thoughts. "It is the realization that the future held the promise of great accomplishment for Joe that made his death so particularly hard for those who knew him. . . . His life as he lived, and finally as he died, could hardly have been improved upon. And through it all, he had a deep and abiding Faith—he was never far from God—and so I cannot help but feel that . . . 'Death to him was less a setting forth than a returning.'"

Peace, Politics, and Power

SAN FRANCISCO'S magnificent Opera House was ablaze with lights. The brilliant colors of the massed flags, the great throngs of world leaders made the opening of the United Nations Conference an exciting adventure.

A reporter for the Hearst-owned International News Service, Jack Kennedy was waiting for the ceremonies to begin. He was also doing some serious thinking. After his discharge from the Navy, he had been at loose ends. He knew he did not want to make the law his career, although he had considered entering Yale Law School after his Harvard graduation. His prewar graduate work at Stanford University convinced him that business was not for him.

Jack's previous success in writing encouraged him to try newspaper work. But the longer he lived the life of a reporter, the more he realized he wanted to *make* news, not just tell about it. He didn't want to *report* history—he wanted to *make* history!

Jack longed to discuss his future with his father. But the tragic death of Joe Jr. had been a severe shock to Mr. Kennedy. For weeks, he had seemed unable to rouse himself, to take any interest in the world around him.

In an effort to be helpful to Jack, however, the elder Kennedy urged his son to think seriously about a political career. Jack needed little urging. Politics was in his Irish blood. The Congressional seat of James Michael Curley, Democrat, was vacant in 1946. John Fitzgerald Kennedy wanted to run for that seat!

The professional politicians paid little attention to the shy, thin, freckle-faced young man, but this did not bother him. Instead of trying to get inside the smoked-filled back rooms of partisan politics, Jack Kennedy walked the streets of the Eleventh Congressional District in an unheard-of door-to-door campaign.

The Kennedy-Fitzgerald name was a magic combination that opened Irish doors and hearts. Since Cambridge was part of the district, Jack's Harvard friends also helped. But the old pros in Boston's Democratic wards roared with laughter when Jack enlisted the help of his former Choate roommate, Lem Billings. For Billings was a Protestant and a Republican! What could he do to help a Catholic and a Democrat in Irish Boston?

Ward heelers felt the same way when they saw redheaded Paul Fay arrive from the West Coast to help his old Navy buddy. Jack's former

PT boat crew arrived in force. And then, of course, there was the family!

"Oh, that family!" Afterwards, when the pros were wondering what hit them, no one could agree whether it had been Jack's remarkable family or his friends that had been their undoing! But no matter how anyone helped, it was Jack Kennedy himself who shook the hands, rang the doorbells, stood outside factory gates to meet the workers. It was Jack who talked to the people and listened to their problems.

When the election returns showed victory, Grandpa Fitzgerald danced an Irish jig and sang "Sweet Adeline" at the campaign headquarters. Jack was in! Representative Kennedy was to stay in, too, through several campaigns that successfully returned him to Washington.

When John F. Kennedy took his seat in the House in January of 1947, he was 29 years old. With his shy, boyish smile, his unruly shock of

JOHN F. **KENNEDY** for CONGRESS.

hair, and his lean, lanky frame, he looked years younger. In his first week on the Hill, the young Congressman was frequently mistaken for a Capitol page boy.

Wearing a dark suit similar to those worn by a page, Jack walked down the aisle of the House one day to take his seat.

A veteran Congressman snapped his fingers at him and demanded a copy of a bill.

Kennedy smiled politely, "Where do I get it?"

The old-timer scowled and bellowed, "How long you been a page, son?"

Jack couldn't control his mirth. While the elderly gentleman fumed, the younger man doubled up with laughter. Jack managed to say, "Sir, I'm a Congressman. From Massachusetts."

One morning, Jack burst into his office, filled with mock indignation. "Can you imagine? Some tourists got into the elevator and asked me to take them to the fourth floor!"

His secretary looked at him with an amused smile and made no comment. Following the direction of her eyes, Kennedy looked down at his old khaki pants, his rumpled seersucker coat, with his shirttail hanging out.

Sheepishly, he said, "I know just what you're thinking! No self-respecting elevator boy would dare enter these stately halls dressed as I am. He'd lose his job!"

His secretary would have been even more amused if she could have seen her boss after hours, hurrying to a near-by Georgetown playground. In an old sweatshirt and sneakers, Jack Kennedy was the center of a gang of boys, white and colored, who had no idea they were catching football passes from a millionaire Congressman.

Kennedy may have been young in looks, but he was maturing politically. The voters liked and trusted him, yet nearly everyone was astonished when he decided to run for the Senate in 1952. His opponent would be the incumbent Senator, popular Henry Cabot Lodge. Senator Lodge was a "Proper Bostonian" from a family long prominent in Massachusetts. It had been his grandfather who had soundly trounced "Honey-Fitz" when that "Irish upstart" ran for Governor.

Again Kennedy started campaigning ahead of the opposition. While Henry Cabot Lodge was boosting Eisenhower for President, Jack covered Massachusetts with family and friends solidly behind him. The dynamic Kennedy sisters and their beautiful mother showed a brand of petti-coat politics that proved devastating to the Republicans. In a race that had been considered political suicide, John F. Kennedy became the Senator from Massachusetts.

"And," said his proud father, "A Kennedy-Fitzgerald beat a *Lodge!*"

Jack had been a Congressman when he first

met Jacqueline Bouvier. Her rare combination of grace, beauty, and intelligence ended the Senator's bachelor days. The wedding of the year, society columnists called the marriage. Her stepfather's Newport mansion was filled with 1200 guests from the social, financial, and political worlds.

Handicapped by ill health for most of his life, Jack Kennedy now found himself in agony with his bad back. Doctors were hesitant to risk surgery, but the Senator insisted. He would not, he said, live his life as a cripple.

The delicate operation was performed. Twice his condition was considered critical, and twice his great will to live pulled him through.

During the long weeks of convalescence, Senator Kennedy read and studied. With the help of Mrs. Kennedy and his aide, Ted Sorenson, a brilliant young Nebraska lawyer, he began the research for a series of articles which would eventually become the Pulitzer-prize-winning book, *Profiles of Courage.*

Once his health was restored to normal, young Kennedy set out to prove himself a capable legislator. As the 1956 Democratic convention rolled around, his name was mentioned as a possible running mate for Presidential candidate Adlai Stevenson. Jack lost the nomination for the Vice Presidential spot by a hair.

This was the turning point in his political career. From that 1956 convention, the Kennedy bandwagon started to roll. Although Jack had three strikes against him—youth, inexperience, and religion—he met each of these issues head on. He sold himself to the public.

In 1960, after a fierce struggle, he won the Democratic nomination for the Presidency. As his running mate, he chose his chief contender, Lyndon Baines Johnson.

Organization, family, and school loyalties, a

superb sense of timing, and political shrewdness, plus an unlimited campaign fund, all worked together for Jack Kennedy's success. Yet, in the final analysis, it was Kennedy himself who won the voters and the votes.

"Lend me your hands and your hearts," he told Americans. "Join me on the New Frontier."

The election in November was one of the closest in the history of the United States. John Fitzgerald Kennedy became President by what the old pros would call "a handful of votes."

United in the President-elect was the boy who loved history and the man who wanted to make history. It was that boy and man who walked in solitude on the dunes at Hyannisport on election eve. It was he who jubilantly sailed his boat on Nantucket Sound the morning after elections. He remembered with a smile that he had named the boat "Victura" because it had something to do with winning!

"Let Us Begin"

THE STIRRING notes of the "Star-Spangled Banner" echoed over Washington. Sharp gusts of wind ruffled the snowdrifts on the Capitol grounds. The air had a frosty bite even in the shelter of the Inaugural Platform.

Dwight D. Eisenhower, oldest President to serve in office, was ready to hand the reins of government to John F. Kennedy, youngest man ever to be elected to the Presidency.

The Inaugural ceremonies began.

Speaker of the House Sam Rayburn administered the oath of office to his fellow Texan, Lyndon Baines Johnson, the new Vice President.

154

The Chief Justice of the United States, Earl Warren, arose and the President-elect stepped forward. Over the Fitzgerald family Bible, John Fitzgerald Kennedy repeated the Oath of Office in a crisp, clear voice.

The 35th President of the United States struck the tone for his Administration in the first moments of the Presidency. "Let the word go forth from this time and place, to friend and foe alike, that the torch has been passed to a new generation of Americans—born in this century, tempered by war, disciplined by a hard and bitter peace, proud of our ancient heritage——"

The eloquent voice continued, "Let every nation know, whether it wishes us well or ill, that we shall pay any price, bear any burden, meet any hardship, support any friend, oppose any foe to assure the survival and the success of liberty."

Applause interrupted again and again.

"All this will not be finished in the first hun-

dred days. Nor will it be finished in the first thousand days, nor in the life of this Administration, nor even perhaps in our lifetime on this planet. But *let us begin*."

John F. Kennedy was America's first Twentieth-Century President. The nation, reflecting its new leader, had a new look. Not since the days of the New Deal and F.D.R. had Washington seen so many bright young men. The White House became a showplace for the nation's art and artists. Poetry and painting were recognized as powerful forces. The sense and the symbols of culture were everywhere.

America's "First Family" became headline stuff. In spite of the First Lady's wish to keep the children out of the limelight, Caroline's antics amused millions. Even John-John's first steps were sensational news.

Touch football became a national pastime. Sailing and water-skiing and fifty-mile hikes became popular. Even rocking chairs became a fad. One political observer was heard to remark, "Any Administration that can turn a rocking chair into a symbol of vigor and vitality can do anything."

The work of the President is a deadly serious business on which the fate of millions of people around the world depends. Yet, with all the necessary sense of purpose and dedication, the White House has its human side, too.

At the first reception for the diplomatic corps, Caroline helped greet the guests in a party dress. "It's my very best one," she confided to her admirers. Every diplomat in Washington will remember Caroline standing on the red carpet in The White House foyer, listening to the Marine Band, her feet tapping in time to the music. When the Band's conductor granted Caroline a request number, she asked for "Old MacDonald Had a Farm." The conductor choked but quickly regained his composure. Never before had that particular tune been played with such polish and style!

The White House, famous for its formal receptions, could be informal, too. There was the day, for example, when Caroline bounced into the press room unexpectedly.

A reporter, idly hoping for a mild scoop, asked, "What's your Daddy doing?"

"Oh, he's upstairs," Caroline replied, "with his shoes and socks off. Just doing nothing."

Even the First Family wasn't immune to the "telephonitis"! According to Grandfather Joseph Kennedy, he was phoning Caroline from Palm Beach. In the background, the elder Kennedy could hear the President of the United States saying, "Hurry up, Caroline, I want to use that telephone."

The Kennedy wit had long been legendary. Now it was still refreshing, still spontaneous.

"I used to wonder," he said once, "when I was a member of the House, how President Truman got into so much trouble. Now that I'm President," he added, with a broad grin, "I'm beginning to get the idea. It's not difficult at all."

Another wry comment came from his relations with an uncooperative Congress. "I never realized how powerful the Senate was until I left it and came up to this end of Pennsylvania Avenue."

As always, he continued to rib his younger brother, Bobby. According to an article in a weekly news magazine, Robert Kennedy was rated the second most powerful man in the nation. Shortly after reading it, President Kennedy commented on the article to his brother.

"Well, Bobby," he said, "there's only one way you can go now. *Down!*"

But behind the quick and ready wit, the Irish charm and gay spirit, was a deeply sincere and purposeful man who loved America and her people. A close observer of the political scene said of the new President, "He is capable, he is dedicated. He's the best-trained man to become President in this century."

The first official trip outside the country was across the friendly frontier to Canada. The President and Mrs. Kennedy were greeted grandly by the Canadian Prime Minister and an elite corps of scarlet-coated Mounties.

At Ottawa's Government House, the President was asked to plant a tree in commemoration of the visit. As he took the silver shovel and bent over, he felt a sharp blinding pain. The photographers and reporters noticed nothing. The President did not make the slightest wince.

But, as Jack Kennedy felt the dull familiar ache tormenting him again, he thought of all the demands and responsibilities that lay ahead. The bad back that had plagued him since his college days, that had racked him with pain when he was injured in the South Pacific, and for which he had undergone major surgery in 1955, was once more his enemy.

However, immediate plans were made for the

President and Mrs. Kennedy to take a European trip which would include a conference with President de Gaulle in Paris and a meeting with Soviet Premier Khrushchev in Vienna.

John F. Kennedy spent his 44th birthday in Hyannisport, quietly resting and studying for his European trip. (Kennedy's youth amazed the Europeans. At 44, he was young enough to be the son of any of the aging world leaders.)

White House Physician Dr. Janet Travelle prescribed special treatment for the painful back condition, which still persisted. Although crutches relieved the strain, Kennedy insisted that he would not be seen on crutches in public—neither before nor during the vitally important European visit. Only the members of the family and the ever-present Secret Service were aware that the President of the United States was a temporary invalid, hobbling about on crutches.

As all the world knows, the Kennedy trip to

Paris was a bonanza of popularity and good-will. A million Frenchmen greeted the handsome couple on the route from Orly Airport to the city. Trumpets sounded at the Elysée Palace.

Both the President and Mrs. Kennedy plunged immediately into the round of activities, the schedule of talks. All that day in the grueling and demanding routine of official functions, John Kennedy was never once seen to limp or slump. Yet his back was giving him severe trouble.

Lem Billings, who was in Paris with the Presidential party, recognized the symptoms. Billings, the President's closest friend since his early teens, never failed to marvel at Jack's ability to endure pain without complaint.

In all the years he had been associated with Kennedy, as boy and man, Billings could not recall any period when Jack had really enjoyed normal health. Yet neither he nor anyone else could recall hearing Jack Kennedy complain.

All of Paris was enchanted with the Kennedys. America's First Lady charmed everyone with her beauty and regal bearing. The French exclaimed, *"Elle est plus reine que toutes les reines"* —She is more queenly than all the queens!

But it was a teen-age advice column in a Paris newspaper which gave Mrs. Kennedy the highest compliment. "All young girls who want to be beautiful should practice sitting and standing gracefully. Then they should look at Jacqueline Kennedy, the example!"

The last evening in France was a brilliant one set in the splendor of the Palace of Versailles. They dined with 150 other guests in the Hall of Mirrors. Here, where French rulers had once lived, history was everywhere.

President de Gaulle bade farewell to America's young leader on the steps of the Elysée Palace. The General said, "Now I have more confidence in your country."

Paris had been three days of enjoyment. Vienna would be different—much different. Premier Khrushchev and President Kennedy met at the American Ambassador's Residence. The talks began immediately and continued throughout the day. Neither fruitful nor fruitless, the conference appeared to be a stalemate, a draw. Yet it served several purposes to President Kennedy. He recognized that the Soviet Premier was not the roly-poly clown of the cartoons. On the contrary, the Russian dictator was a well-informed, alert, proud, and extremely formidable adversary.

During the grim business of discussing the future of the world, President Kennedy was able to hold his own. As well informed on each issue as the Russian leader, Kennedy also showed great patience and sense of purpose.

As the time came for the discussions to close, the tension was marked. There had been no agreements, no concessions, no deals. Formal farewells were said with unsmiling faces.

Air Force One, the President's jet, sped toward London and still another conference. President Kennedy reported to Prime Minister MacMillan and the London visit was climaxed by dining at Buckingham Palace with the Queen.

Back in the States, the President talked to the American people immediately over a nation-wide network. "I went to Vienna to meet the leader of the Soviet Union. It was a very sober two days . . . We have wholly different views of right and wrong, of what is an internal affair and what is aggression, and above all, we have wholly different concepts of where the world is and where it is going."

John Kennedy concluded his message to his fellow Americans by saying, "But with the will and the work, freedom will prevail."

President Kennedy's New Frontier was

marked by triumphs as well as by defeats and stalemate. Yet he never gave up hope of success. Again and again, he said, "We can, I believe, solve a good many of our problems. They are man-made and they can be solved by man."

In June of 1963, President Kennedy was bound for Europe once more. In Germany, the young leader was cheered from Bonn to Frankfurt and on to Berlin. In West Berlin, two million enthusiastic Germans stood ten to twenty deep to glimpse the President of the United States.

When the Presidential car reached the Brandenburg Gate and the Berlin Wall, John Kennedy stared in silence. He clenched and unclenched his fist as he saw the infamous Wall. No longer smiling, he looked at the dead waste, at the ugly, barren city of East Berlin.

The President brought a reassuring message to the thousands of West Germans massed in front of Berlin's City Hall.

"Your liberty is our liberty," he said. With deep emotion, he added, "There are many people in the world who really don't understand—or say they don't—what is the real issue between the free world and the communist world. Let them come to Berlin! There are some who say that communism is the wave of the future. Let them come to Berlin!"

Later that week on his visit to Ireland, John Fitzgerald Kennedy stood on the New Ross Quay from which his great-grandfather sailed to America. "Welcome home" said the signs and the Irish crowds echoed the words.

"I am glad to be here," Jack Kennedy said. "It took three generations, one hundred and fifteen years and six thousand miles to make this trip. When my great-grandfather left the Old World for the New, he carried nothing with him to America except two things, a strong religious faith and a strong desire for liberty. I am glad to say that all of his great-grandchildren have valued that inheritance."

The autumn of 1963 saw the President lead America toward a great step for peace. In early October, the Nuclear Test Ban Treaty was signed after its ratification by the Senate. To John F. Kennedy, this marked the most gratifying achievement of his Administration.

The President could now turn to domestic affairs. Earlier in the fall, two Westerners, Secretary of the Interior Udall of Arizona and New Mexico's Senator Anderson had urged him to make a conservation tour. Because of the remarkable success of the Western trip, Southern political leaders asked the President to make a good will tour of the South.

The third week in November started out to be the kind of political crusade which John Kennedy enjoyed. On Monday, he spoke to several audiences in Florida. He flew back to

Washington for two days of official business before departing again for another political safari.

This trip would take the President and Mrs. Kennedy to Texas. It began, as so many others had before it, on the South lawn of The White House. John-John and Caroline said goodbye as the Marine helicopter arrived to pick up their father and mother, and take them to the airport.

The President's visit to the Lone Star State was primarily for political reasons, to help hold Texas for the Democrats in 1964. The receptions in San Antonio, Houston, and Fort Worth were all warm and enthusiastic.

John Fitzgerald Kennedy looked forward to the next day when he would once again take to the campaign trail that he loved so much. The date would be Friday, November 22, and the place would be Dallas.

Beyond the New Frontier

FRIDAY, NOVEMBER twenty-second, dawned gray and gloomy. The clouds over Fort Worth were dark with the threat of rain. But not even the persistent drizzle could discourage the crowd of Texans gathered to see the President.

Jack Kennedy walked out of the hotel with his familiar buoyant stride. Hatless in spite of the rain, he looked around the crowded parking lot and smiled his obvious enjoyment.

"There are no faint hearts in Fort Worth. I appreciate your being here this morning."

In response to a disappointed murmur from those hoping to see the First Lady, he said, "Mrs.

172

Kennedy is organizing herself." There was a burst of laughter and he continued, "It takes her longer, but of course, she looks better than we do after she does it!"

This time, the President joined the laughter.

Later, at the Chamber of Commerce breakfast, he was in top form. His speech was well received. After special presentations and further good humor, the Presidential party boarded the plane for the next stop—Dallas.

The drizzling rain was left behind. The sun was golden in the blue Texas sky when Air Force One set down at Love Field. The President and Mrs. Kennedy were welcomed enthusiastically. Governor Connally and Vice President Johnson surveyed the scene with pleasure. The Texas trip was going perfectly!

The motorcycles roared impatiently. The President seated himself in the Lincoln limousine beside Mrs. Kennedy. Because it was a sunny, beautiful day, he decided against using the bullet-proof top.

For a supposedly unfriendly and dangerous city, Dallas was giving a rousing welcome to the Kennedys. Cheering Texans jammed the sidewalks and spilled out into the street. The lead motorcycles rolled toward downtown Dallas.

As the President turned to wave at the people thronging the curb, the Governor's lady smiled at him over her shoulder. "You can't say Dallas isn't friendly to you today!"

The President laughed and started to reply.

His answer was stilled, forever stilled, by the sharp crack of a rifle——

Friday, November twenty-second! The President of the United States was assassinated! Across the nation and around the world, flags flew at half mast. In a thousand cities, towns, and villages, bells began to toll.

All over the globe, America's grief was felt

and shared. Great names and common people alike mourned our leader as their own. There was a shocked sadness, not only for what President Kennedy was, but even more for what he might have been. John F. Kennedy's death was particularly tragic because it came at the beginning, not at the end, of his career.

The world will long remember the poise and self-control of the President's widow. Never to be forgotten was the contained grief of the President's family. This tragedy marked the third violent death the Kennedys had known. Joe Jr. had been killed in action in 1944. Their beloved Kick had died in a plane crash in 1948. Now, the assassination was a dreadful climax. Yet Rose Kennedy had borne each death with courage and grace, with a mother's love and heartache.

Church bells tolled on Sunday morning, November twenty-fourth. Along Pennsylvania Avenue came the roll of muffled drums, as John

Fitzgerald Kennedy left The White House for his last journey up to Capitol Hill.

The same horse-drawn caisson that carried the coffin of President Roosevelt eighteen years before moved slowly up the Avenue. Behind the Presidential flag followed a riderless horse. From the empty saddle hung a black-handled sword in a silver scabbard. A pair of boots was reversed in the stirrups, signifying that a commander had fallen and would never rise again.

When the slow cortege arrived at the Capitol, the Navy Band played "Hail to the Chief." Cannon boomed a twenty-one gun salute for the President. Because Jack Kennedy loved the Navy, the Band played the solemn Navy Hymn, "Eternal Father."

Military pall bearers, representing each one of the services, carried the casket of their Commander-in-Chief into the Rotunda of the Capitol. The President lay in state with an honor guard.

A quarter of a million people waited in line throughout the long afternoon and all through the chill of the night to pay their respects.

Final ceremonies for President Kennedy were observed on Monday, November twenty-fifth. The last religious rites were held at St. Matthew's Cathedral. The cadence of the muffled drums throbbed through the city, measuring a sad, slow pace for the procession to the church.

Following the flag-draped caisson was the President's widow, walking with his two brothers, Attorney General Robert Kennedy and Senator Edward Kennedy. The marching mourners numbered two hundred of the world's leaders, the greatest congress of foreign dignitaries ever in Washington. Emperor and Queen, Presidents and Prime Ministers walked side by side.

Also walking to the Cathedral was America's new President, Lyndon Baines Johnson, with

178

Mrs. Johnson, the new First Lady. Urged by Secret Service men to ride to the funeral, President Johnson replied, "I'd rather give my life than be afraid to give it."

Waiting at the Cathedral were the two men who had led the nation before John F. Kennedy —former Presidents Eisenhower and Truman.

Richard Cardinal Cushing, the intimate friend of the Kennedy family who had presided at the wedding of the President and spoken at the President's Inauguration, officiated at the funeral. At the Altar of St. Matthew's, he celebrated the Requiem Mass. "May the angels, dear Jack, lead you into Paradise." For the next few moments, countless millions paused to honor the President of the United States. Memorial services were held all over the world.

As the honor guard took the coffin back out into the sunshine, the band struck up "Hail to the Chief." On the Cathedral steps, Caroline held fast to her mother's hand and brushed a tear away. John-John, who was three years old this same day of his father's funeral, saw the flag on the casket and saluted in a touching gesture.

At Arlington's National Cemetery, the headstones mark the last resting place of those men who have served their Country. Only one other President, William Howard Taft, had been buried at Arlington. In a way, Jack Kennedy had unknowingly suggested the site himself. A few months before, he had slipped over to Arlington for a breath of air. Looking out over the magnificent view of Washington, he said, "I could stay up here forever!"

At the graveside service, bagpipes wailed their mournful tune as the pipers from the Air Force marched past. Overhead, fifty jet aircraft, one for each State of the Union, streaked through the sky. The apex of the last V formation was empty, symbolizing a fallen leader. The President's personal plane, Air Force One, trailed the formation, dipping its wings in a final tribute.

A twenty-one gun salute boomed in the distance, the last for our 35th President. Up on the hill, three musket volleys cracked. A bugle sounded its first lonely note. The bugler faltered, then the haunting sadness of taps echoed on the air.

The sloping hillside of Arlington looks out over the Washington that was John F. Kennedy's New Frontier. The Avenue of Heroes leads straight across the Potomac to the Lincoln Memorial. Beyond it, the Washington Monument towers toward the sky. In the far distance, the dome of the United States Capitol is a shining landmark by day and night.

During the twilight hours of that November twenty-fifth, planes took off for all the corners of the earth, returning the world's leaders to their native lands, taking Americans home.

One of these planes was bound for the New England that Jack Kennedy had loved as a boy and represented as a man. As his flight took off over the Capitol at dusk, Seymour St. John, the Headmaster of the Choate School, wrote a tribute to a famous alumnus, to John F. Kennedy.

"Take off across the silver river,
    Washington's Potomac, Lincoln's,
    Kennedy's now; and on it flows.

Others fell that day—ten thousands
    Died November 22nd;
    And some were old, some very young,
    But only one was forty-six.

The Capitol shines white below;
    The marble halls of government
    Stand out against their drabber neighbors.
    These were his; he gave them life,
    And they gave back vitality.
    Can it be true he's wrenched away?
    That all these forums of a week
    Ago are silenced, lifeless left?

The sunset afterglow behind
The wing makes fiery western skies.
Ahead it's dark. The streets beneath,
Lamp-lighted now, blind alleys start
And wander off to nothingness.

What's left to us? God help us think:
His humor, warmth—these can't be
                                    crushed.
His vision of a world made free,
His faith in reason, hope for country,
All that we believe in, shared;
His hate of prejudice, of strife.

But look: there shines the evening star.
What has he left to us?
                    His life."

Hail to the Chief!

THE BABBLE of young voices rose to a din, then quieted down as the teacher entered. The class in Public Affairs was meeting in the school library. Students for this new course in American Government had been carefully chosen from fifth- and sixth-graders.

The boys and girls listened intently to the teacher. "The discussion topic for today is the Presidency of the United States. Last week, the class agreed to choose one feature of this huge topic to talk about. What's your choice?"

A boy in a football jersey answered. "No matter what happens to the *man* who is Presi-

184

dent, the *office* of President continues. We wanted to learn more about this."

"Excellent!" The teacher approved.

A girl in the front row said, "There's terrific information about the Presidency in our library —books, magazines, and papers."

The boy sitting next to her agreed. "One magazine was published by the United States Information Service just after the assassination of President Kennedy. It's called 'The President of the United States of America' and it shows just how our country carries on after a national tragedy or emergency."

During the discussion that followed, the boys and girls learned that in many countries around the globe, the sudden death of the head of state or the assassination of the political leader would result in public chaos. The government might be taken over by a rival political power or the armed forces might revolt.

Not so in America. President Kennedy's death, tragic though it was, proved that our government is a remarkably shock-proof system. A crisis that would have been fatal to most governments simply served to unite Americans.

Seven times before that fatal November 22nd of 1963, an American President had died while still in office. (Three of those times had been by an assassination.) Seven times before, the office of President had been immediately filled by the Vice President. This was the law of the land, the law of the United States of America, provided for in a one-sentence clause of the Constitution of 1787. Just as our founding fathers ordained centuries ago, Vice President Lyndon Baines Johnson became President.

"Here's a clipping that brings out this continuity of the Presidency," another boy volunteered. "It's dated November 25, 1963, the same day President Kennedy was buried at Arlington.

'A Legacy of Courage' is the title of an editorial in *The Christian Science Monitor*."

"Please read it," the teacher asked.

"It begins with a quotation from another Congressman who became President, just as John Kennedy did," the boy explained.

" ' "Fellow citizens! God reigns and the Government at Washington still lives!"

" 'With these words, James A. Garfield, then a young Congressman with an outstanding war record, reassured the people after the assassination of President Lincoln.

" 'Fifteen years later, President Garfield himself succumbed to the effects of a bullet fired by a disgruntled office seeker. But then, again, "the Government at Washington" lived on!' "

The boy paused. "I'll skip a little to save time. The next part says, 'John F. Kennedy served his country in this tradition. He had a warm feeling for everyday people and was warmly loved by them. He gave unstintingly of the best of his abilities in behalf of the public good. He brought able men into the government and led them with courage.' "

When the teacher asked for other information, a boy in Scout uniform suggested, "There was an article on the Presidency and on John F. Kennedy in *Boy's Life* for February, 1964. This isn't in the school library, but I have a copy."

"Read a few lines," the teacher suggested.

"The article is by Bob Hood," the boy explained, as he started to read. " 'In the gloom of that grim weekend last November, there were things to be proud of. Through its grief and through the presence of its great leaders at the funeral, the world paid respect not only to a fine man but to the Presidency itself, an office which has great meaning to all people. Although an assassin cut down the President, the Presidency lived on, as always.' "

The boy turned the page and read on. " 'We should all take pride in our government, in how it pulled together in crisis, reassuring its citizens and people of the free world that the Union stood firm. We should take pride that our nation did not falter, that it continues in the spirit of President Kennedy's Inaugural Address: *With a good conscience our only sure reward, with history the final judge of our deeds, let us go forth to lead the land we love, asking His blessings and His help but knowing that here on earth, God's work must truly be our own.*' "

"This is a remarkable collection of quotations," the teacher said. "Any others?"

"President Johnson spoke to the nation on Thanksgiving Day in 1963, a few days after the assassination." The girl in the front row spoke up again. "He said, 'A great leader is dead. A great nation must move on. Yesterday is not ours to recover, but tomorrow is ours to win or lose. . . .

A deed that was meant to tear us apart has bound us together.'"

"You boys and girls have certainly given this topic much thought," the teacher said. "Any other comments?"

"Yes, please," a girl on the far side of the room said shyly. "I'd like to share some words of President Kennedy's that aren't very well known. He spoke at a small gathering in South Carolina the same year as his death and I'll never forget his words: 'A man may die, nations rise and fall, but an idea lives on. Ideas have endurance without death.'"

The library was hushed and quiet.

"An idea lives on." The teacher broke the silence. "No thought could more eloquently express the Presidency of the United States!" He cleared his throat and said, "Like all great Americans, President Kennedy will live on in the words and works which he left behind. Many of our past Presidents have been honored by memorials and monuments. We're all familiar with the Washington Monument and the Lincoln Memorial. Today, there are Kennedy memorials everywhere—in our national capital, throughout America, and around the world. But no monument could be a greater honor to any President

than the Presidential Medal of Freedom which was awarded posthumously to John F. Kennedy."

The room was quiet except for the sound of the teacher's voice. "President Johnson read this citation in ceremonies at The White House on December 6, 1963. 'John Fitzgerald Kennedy, 35th President of the United States, soldier, scholar, statesman, defender of freedom, pioneer for peace, author of hope—combining courage with reason and combatting hate with compassion, he led the land he loved toward new frontiers of opportunity for all men and peace for all time. Beloved in a life of selfless service, mourned by all in a death of senseless crime, the energy, faith and devotion which he brought to his extraordinarily successful though tragically brief endeavor will hereafter *light our country and all who serve it—and the glow from that fire can truly light the world.*' "